Coast to Coast
Discoveries

Our Canada

Coast to Coast

Discoveries

Reader's Digest Association (Canada) ULC
Project Staff
Contributing Editor Robert Ronald
Senior Art Designer Andrée Payette
Assistant Designer Ann Devoe
Production Coordinator Gillian Sylvain
Manager, English Book Editorial Pamela Johnson
Vice-President, Editorial Robert Goyette
Managing Editor, *Our Canada* and *More of Our Canada* Gary George

The Reader's Digest Association, Inc.
President & CEO Robert Guth
Executive Vice President, RDA & President, North America Dan Lagani
Executive Vice President, RDA & President, Allrecipes.com Lisa Sharples
Executive Vice President, RDA & President, Europe Dawn Zier

Produced by Toucan Books Ltd.
Managing Director Ellen Dupont
Editor Theresa Bebbington
Picture Research Christine Vincent and Sharon Southren
Designer Dave Jones
Proofreader Marion Dent
Indexer Michael Dent

Text by Cynthia O'Brien, Lisa Halvorsen and Joe Yogerst

Additional fact checking: Valerie Nobert

Map by Cartographics, Ltd.

Copyright 2012 Toucan Books Ltd.

OUR CANADA, COAST TO COAST DISCOVERIES
Published by *Our Canada*, an imprint of the Reader's Digest Association (Canada), ULC
© 2012 by Reader's Digest Association (Canada), ULC
© 2012 by The Reader's Digest Association, Inc.
© 2012 by Reader's Digest Association Far East Ltd.
Philippine © 2012 by The Reader's Digest Association Far East Ltd.

Library and Archives Canada Cataloguing in Publication

Our Canada : coast to coast discoveries : over 350 Canadian dream destinations to see and visit / the editors of Reader's Digest.

Includes index.
ISBN 978-1-55475-110-5 (hardcover)
ISBN 978-1-55267-928-9 (paperback)

1. Canada--Guidebooks. I. Reader's Digest Association (Canada)

FC38.O87 2012   917.104'73   C2012-900310-7

Note: The editors have taken reasonable measures to confirm the accuracy of the information in this book. Information that will enable the publisher to rectify errors in future printings will be welcome.

We are committed to both the quality of our products and the service we provide to our customers. If you have any comments about the content of this book, please write to:
The Book Editor, Reader's Digest Association (Canada) ULC,
1100 René-Lévesque Blvd. W., Montreal, QC H3B 5H5

For more Our Canada products and information, visit our website at
www.ourcanada.ca
  and
For more Reader's Digest products and information, visit our website at
www.readersdigest.ca

Contents

Foreword

As every Canadian knows, there's an amazing array of places to see and things to do within the borders of this great land of ours. You've probably come across many during your travels in Canada and, if asked, I bet you could also sing the praises of all the wonderful spots to visit in your own neck of the woods. Add to these the countless Canadian locales you've seen on TV, happened upon on the Internet or read about— quite possibly in the pages of *Our Canada* and *More of Our Canada* magazines—and you end up with an impressive list of Canadian travel destinations with which you are familiar. Even taking all you're aware of into account, we're barely scratching the surface of all the fabulous places that are just waiting to be discovered right here in our own country. That's where *Our Canada, Coast to Coast Discoveries* comes in most handy.

Within the following pages, you'll be taken on a photography-rich scenic tour of the Canada you know and love, as well as the Canada you've yet to visit. Travelling along the familiar highways and byways of your home province or territory, you'll hopefully nod with approval at the mix of established attractions and off-the-beaten-track "must see" stops that are highlighted. Combined with the helpful tips, suggestions and snippets of history and background information that are built into the very fabric of this book, you'll come away with an even deeper appreciation of what makes your corner of the country so special. And the same applies for the Canadian destinations you may have already encountered; in fact, based on your discoveries here, don't be surprised if you find yourself tempted to return to a previous haunt or two.

However, being thoroughly introduced to the parts of Canada that you've yet to experience firsthand is where *Our Canada, Coast to Coast Discoveries* truly excels. Stunning photography, town and city profiles, dozens of feature topics, tidbits from the locals, at-a-glance listings and "if-you-decide-to-go" travel advice make this book a keeper for the person who is planning to hit the road soon and the armchair traveller alike. I hope you enjoy it as much as I did.

Gary George, Managing Editor,
Our Canada and *More of Our Canada*

NOTE: If after enjoying this book, you find yourself out there exploring Canada— from its rugged wilderness and picturesque rural settings to its diverse cultural communities and major urban centres, remember to send your stories and photos to us at ourcanada.ca. You just might see your great Canadian adventure published within the travel pages of the country's favourite reader-written magazines: *Our Canada* and *More of Our Canada*.

Icons Inside the Book

Below is a key to the icons found within the entries in the book. These provide at-a-glance information on specific attractions available at the sites.

🌲 Nature park or forest

👫 Site of interest for children

🏛 Museum or historic building

🪑 Tranquil setting

🖼 Art gallery

🐦 Birdwatching

⛷ Winter sports

⛵ Boating

🐟 Fishing

ATLANTIC
CANADA

Around Newfoundland and Labrador

ST. JOHN'S

The oldest and most easterly city in North America, St. John's rich history dates back to 1497, when Italian explorer John Cabot sailed into its harbour. Once a major trade port for Newfoundland and Labrador and the largest supplier of salt cod in the world, today its harbour still teems with cargo vessels and cruise ships. Icebergs and whales pass by in silent splendour in spring and early summer. Hilly residential streets are filled with clapboard row houses painted in crayon-coloured hues, a tradition stemming back to the days when sailing ships went to sea for long periods of time. When returning to port the captains would find it easy to spot their own home while still a long way from shore.

Signal Hill provides the best view of the picturesque harbour. Guglielmo Marconi received the first transatlantic wireless transmission here, and the hill also played a major role in harbour defence until the Second World War. Cabot Tower, with exhibits on military and communications history, was built in 1897 to commemorate the 400th anniversary of the explorer's arrival.

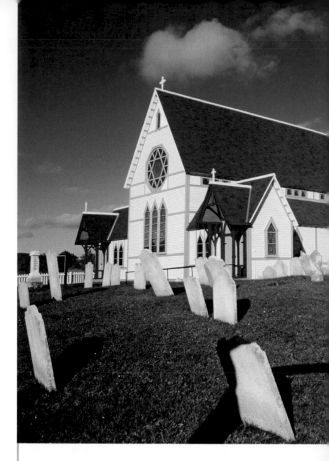

Trinity St. Paul's Anglican Church, a delightful 19th-century Gothic revival-style church, overlooks the historic town of Trinity and Trinity Harbour.

The drive to the top of Signal Hill passes the Johnson Geo Centre, where exhibits focus on the geology of the earth and the sinking of the RMS *Titanic* about 565 kilometres off Newfoundland and Labrador's coast.

The Quidi Vidi Battery Provincial Historic Site, a reconstruction of the battery that the British took from the French, overlooks Quidi Vidi village, one of St. John's prettiest neighbourhoods. It's home to the annual St. John's Regatta and to Mallard Cottage, the oldest cottage in North America, built in the 1750s.

Cobblestoned George Street, closed to traffic at night, has many lively pubs and restaurants. The focal point of the city's arts

Signal Hill Tattoo Visit the hilltop in peak summer months to experience a 19th-century re-enactment full of colour, pageantry and military drills.

scene is the Resource Centre for the Arts in the LSPU Hall in downtown St. John's.

Cape Spear National Historic Site, just 17 kilometres outside city limits, is the easternmost point on the continent and site of Newfoundland and Labrador's oldest surviving lighthouse. From Bay Bulls, a short drive south of the city, tour boats depart for the Witless Bay Ecological Reserve, a group of offshore islands where Atlantic puffins and other seabirds nest in summer and migrating whales are a common sight.

PLANNING
Music festivals, cultural events and outdoor recreation fill St. John's calendar year-round.
🏘 🏛 🏞 🐦 🦅

TRINITY
Trinity's location on a sheltered, deepwater harbour made it an attractive anchorage for European fishing vessels as early as the 16th century. Later merchant ships arrived from the south of England to deliver salt and supplies and pick up shipments of dried and salted codfish for Europe. The town's history, shaped by its connection to the sea, is chronicled at the Trinity Interpretation Centre and the Trinity Museum, a late 19th-century saltbox-style home, as well as through the Rising Tide Theatre's "New Founde Land," an outdoor pageant that walks ticket holders through town to different locales. Several preserved industrial and commercial buildings, including the Green Family Forge, the Ryan Building (a restored 1820s counting house) and the Lester-Garland Premises Mercantile Building, tell the story of its commercial prosperity and growth. A 10-minute walk to the top of Ryder's Hill, known locally as Gun Hill, affords remarkable views of the town, Trinity Bight and historic Fort Point, once the site of three military installations. The 5.3-kilometre Skerwink Trail, a moderately strenuous cliff hike, promises breathtaking vistas and seabird, whale and iceberg sightings.

PLANNING
Summer is theatre season, while autumn is the ideal time for hiking.
🏛 🏞 🐦 🦅 🌊

CAPE ST. MARY'S
A 1-kilometre walk through meadows, often filled with grazing sheep, and along the top of steep sea cliffs at Cape St. Mary's Ecological Reserve brings birdwatchers to one of the world's largest and most easily accessible seabird rookeries. The site, on the southwestern tip of Avalon Peninsula, is home to an estimated 24,000 northern gannets, 20,000 black-legged kittiwakes, 20,000 common murres and 2,000 thick-billed murres. Black guillemots, razorbill

---

Gannet rookery Northern gannets began nesting on Cape St. Mary's in the late 1800s when hunting and predation on Funk Island forced them to seek a safer haven.

auks and northern fulmars also can be found nesting on Bird Rock, the 100-metre-high sea stack favoured by the gannets, and on the vertical cliff walls nearby. The eye-level bird observation area is only 10 metres from the gannet colony on the rock outcropping, allowing for spectacular viewing of their courtship and feeding behaviours, flying manoeuvres and interactions between parents and chicks. Before the arrival of the gannets in the late 19th century, Cape Mary was best known for its lighthouse and rich offshore fishing grounds. A lighthouse keeper's cottage serves as the interpretive centre, operated by the Newfoundland and Labrador Provincial Park System, where you can see exhibits on northern seabirds and guided tours to the colony begin.

PLANNING
Although the reserve is open year-round, prime viewing time for gannets and other seabirds is May to October, which coincides with the birds' breeding season.
🌲 🏞 🐦

Iceberg Alley Kayaking is one way to see the icebergs, but proceed with caution—only the tip of the iceberg is visible above the waterline.

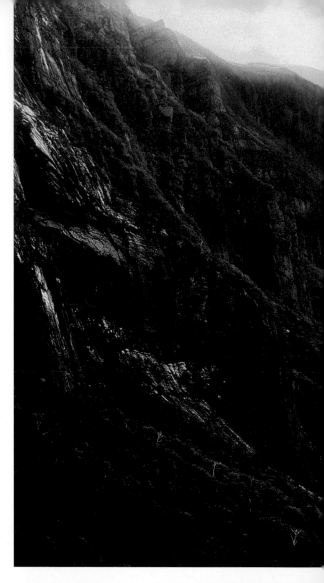

SAINT-PIERRE AND MIQUELON

Located only 20 kilometres off the coast of Newfoundland and Labrador's Burin Peninsula, the islands of Saint-Pierre and Miquelon were claimed for the King of France by Jacques Cartier in 1536. The islands are still ruled by France. Saint-Pierre, the smaller but more populous island, is reminiscent of a French town with its architecture and cafés. Exhibits at the Musée Héritage display the island's history. Miquelon, with about 600 Acadian-descended residents, is more rugged with abundant wildlife. Seals and wild horses share the beaches with shipwrecks and large seabird populations. Migrating whales are commonly spotted off the islands.

PLANNING
Festivals are big in summer when the islands commemorate Bastille Day, July 14, and Jacques Cartier's arrival a few weeks later.
🌲 🏛 🦤

TWILLINGATE

Its location on Notre Dame Bay at the edge of Iceberg Alley puts Twillingate's island community of 2,500 residents in the thick of the action for viewing these mammoth chunks of ice. Trips can be booked for an up-close look or to search for the many whale species, including humpbacks, minkes and sperm whales, that migrate through these waters. Harp seals are common in early summer and shearwaters, Atlantic puffins, black guillemots and other bird species at different times throughout the year. On shore a number of hiking trails, including the Top of Twillingate Trail, an easy two-hour climb to the highest point of land, provide superb vantage points for panoramic views, birdwatching and iceberg spotting.

A handful of museums feature exhibits on historical events, while art galleries carry crafts and artworks by resident artists. Auk Island Winery produces berry wines made with pure iceberg water. The Fish, Fun and Folk Festival Week takes place in late July.

PLANNING
The best time for viewing icebergs and marine wildlife is between May and mid-July.
🌲 🏛 🚣 🖼 ⛵ 🐦

L'Anse aux Meadows

In 1960 archaeologists unearthed evidence at L'Anse aux Meadows, Newfoundland and Labrador's northernmost tip, of 11th-century wood and sod buildings similar to those found in Norse villages in Greenland at the time. The discovery supports long-standing beliefs that the Vikings were the first European settlers in North America. About 2 kilometres from the excavated site, costumed interpreters recreate typical village life at Norstead, a replica of a Viking-era port of trade with full-size buildings, including a chieftain's hall and church and Viking knarrs (ships).

Battle Harbour Once the centre of a thriving fisheries industry in the late 18th and 19th centuries, the town was abandoned when the industry declined.

BATTLE HARBOUR

Once known as the Salt Fish Capital of Labrador, Battle Harbour is located on Battle Island off Labrador's southeastern coast. Today the town has been preserved as the Battle Harbour National Historic District, a stunning example of what coastal Labrador life was like a century ago. Passenger ferry service from Mary's Harbour grants travellers access to the island. Guided walking tours of the district go past once-busy wharves, abandoned shops and private dwellings and up a short hill to St. James the Apostle Church and its adjacent cemetery. This mid-19th-century Anglican church, designed by world-renowned ecclesiastical architect William Grey, is the oldest surviving Anglican church in Labrador. A trail around the island passes by Maritime Archaic Indian archaeological sites, a Second World War plane wreck and other points of interest, including the Marconi Station, where Admiral Robert E. Peary announced the news of his successful North Pole trek. Icebergs, whales, dolphins, seals and seabirds may be observed from the island or on the ferry trip.

PLANNING

Passenger ferry service is available only from mid-June to mid-September when the Battle Harbour National Historic District is open.

GROS MORNE

Atlantic Canada's second largest park, at 1,805 square kilometres, Gros Morne National Park on Newfoundland and Labrador's west coast was designated a UNESCO World Heritage Site in 1987 for its unique geological features, including exposed ocean crust and mantle rock and numerous rock formations. Moose and caribou are commonly spotted along the more than 100 kilometres of hiking trails, along with colourful displays of wildflowers, including wild orchids, in the spring and summer months. Boat trips traverse the 15-kilometre-long Western Brook Pond, the main fjord. A road around Bonne Bay, which splits the park into two sections,

Western Brook Pond Glaciers were responsible for the awe-inspiring fjords, inland lakes and valleys found in mountainous Gros Morne.

affords splendid views of this deep, dark water fjord. Located between the towns of Woody Point and Trout River, the Tablelands rise dramatically to form a barren desertlike landscape. Gros Morne attracts hikers and campers in the warmer months. Winter visitors can snowshoe, snowmobile or ski on groomed or backcountry trails.

PLANNING

The park is a four-season destination; Green Point Campground stays open year-round.

A Dozen Great Seaside Towns

Peggy's Cove, Nova Scotia

Named after the lone survivor of a 19th-century shipwreck off its rocky coast, Peggy's Cove, with its postcard-pretty harbour and striking lighthouse, is one of the most photographed places in Atlantic Canada. The village is located on the eastern point of St. Margaret's Bay, about 45 kilometres southwest of Halifax, along Novia Scotia's Bluenose Coast. The 15-metre-high, white and red octagonal lighthouse stands on a stark granite outcropping overlooking the cold waters of the Atlantic. Built in 1915, it replaced the original 1868 wooden lighthouse. Nearby, working lobster boats wait near weathered piers for the next day's run. Wooden fish sheds, a contrast to the vibrantly coloured houses, line the sheltered waters of Peggy's Cove, a small fishing village first settled in 1811 by six German families. By the early 20th century, the community had 300 residents—which is about five times greater than the community's current population—and a thriving fishing industry, including its own lobster cannery. A 30-metre-high sculpture by marine artist and sculptor William deGarthe, perhaps the village's best known resident, pays homage to Nova Scotia's fishermen and their families. It stands outside the deGarthe Gallery, where more of his works are displayed. Another tribute, this one a memorial to the victims of the 1998 Swissair crash,

Other Great Seaside Towns

Bouctouche, New Brunswick. Le Pays de la Sagouine, a cultural theme park, is a welcoming community on pretty Bouctouche Bay.

Caraquet, New Brunswick. Set on one of the world's most breathtaking bays, this Acadian community has an unmatched joie de vivre for arts, culture and tradition. It hosts one of the most popular Acadian festivals in North America each summer.

St. Martins, New Brunswick. This small fishing village at the gateway to the Fundy Trail Parkway charms visitors with its whispering caves and miles of beaches waiting to be explored.

Shediac, New Brunswick. Known as the "Lobster Capital of the World" and home to the world's largest lobster statue, the popular summer resort town on Shediac Bay holds an annual lobster festival every summer.

Bonavista, Newfoundland and Labrador. Explorer John Cabot's first landfall in Atlantic Canada, Bonavista also celebrates its five centuries of cod fishery at the Ryan Premises National Historic Site, a restored fish merchant's property.

Brigus, Newfoundland and Labrador. This captivating community on Conception Bay was the birthplace of Captain Bob Bartlett, who accompanied Admiral Robert E. Peary on many of his polar expeditions. Hawthorne Cottage National Historical Site, Bartlett's home, is one of several historical buildings in the area.

Chester, Nova Scotia. The influences of New England settlers on the village's many clapboard saltboxes and Cape Cod-style homes make it a favourite set location for miniseries, movies and television shows.

Chéticamp, Nova Scotia. Chéticamp on the Cabot Trail, which skirts the seacoast in northern Cape Breton, embraces the culture, traditions and friendliness of the Acadians.

Lunenburg, Nova Scotia. This picturesque seaport begs to be explored by historic walking tour, whale-watch, lobster boat trip or visit to its expansive Fisheries Museum of the Atlantic.

Mahone Bay, Nova Scotia. The tranquility of Mahone Bay belies its storied past as a hideout for pirates plying local waters. Today it's the ideal hideaway for travellers seeking a quiet escape.

North Rustico, Prince Edward Island. Bordering on Prince Edward Island National Park, this town has a harbour filled with working lobster boats and a small fisheries museum.

can be found just outside the village limits overlooking the area where the plane went down. The region is also a magnet for people interested in active outdoor activities, such as hiking and kayaking, as well as birdwatching and whale-watching.

Planning: Other than the taxis that meet cruise ships, there is little public transportation in the area. Most people drive from Halifax or Yarmouth; for stunning scenery along the way, follow the Lighthouse Route. Accommodations are available, including oceanfront campgrounds as well as bed and breakfast establishments and inns.

The Port City of Halifax

Overlooking the world's second largest natural harbour, vivacious Halifax is no slouch when it comes to cultural, culinary and recreational offerings.

With one foot in the past and the other pointed towards the future, Halifax is a destination that does not disappoint. For a small metropolis, it has a dazzling number of cultural resources—art galleries, professional theatre and museums spinning out stories of its past, including the city's connection to the *Titanic*, one the world's greatest peacetime maritime disasters. Its waterfront boardwalk, the longest in North America, links dining, shopping and entertainment options with heritage sites and parks. While this walkable city is deeply rooted in the past, its festivals, universities and music scene give it a youthful vibe.

On the Waterfront

The Halifax Boardwalk is where street performers entertain, arresting harbour views demand a photo and aromas from restaurants lure visitors in for a quick bite or lingering meal. Stretching ten city blocks in the centre of downtown, it provides easy access to Casino Nova Scotia, the Maritime Museum of the Atlantic and Historic Properties, a restored waterfront warehouse district with boardwalk, restaurants and shops. Daily boat tours of the harbour and for whale-watches depart from Cable Wharf.

Up the hill from the waterfront, the Art Gallery of Nova Scotia, housed in the former Canadian Mounted Police headquarters, displays old masterpieces side by side with works by contemporary Canadian artists. The Old Triangle Irish Alehouse on Prince Street, a popular Halifax nightspot, offers traditional Celtic music and step dancing.

Tracking the Past

At the Citadel, a 19th-century British fort perched on Halifax's highest point, the daily changing of the guard and renovated guardhouse, barracks and other fortifications draw visitors into Halifax's military past. The views of the city and the harbour are impressive, as are the nearby Public Gardens, a quiet oasis in a bustling city since the mid-19th century. Pier 21 provides a poignant look at the lives of the immigrants, Canadian soldiers, war brides and orphans who arrived at this immigration hall in the early to mid-1900s, hoping to get the coveted "Landed Immigrant" stamp on their papers. Halifax's rich history also comes to life at the Atlantic Canada Aviation Museum and the Province House, Nova Scotia's legislature since 1819. The Alexander Keith Brewery, the oldest working brewery in North America, has tours about the beer, the brewery and life in Halifax in the 1860s.

Don't Miss

Halifax Seaport Farmers' Market
More than 200 vendors sell fresh produce, cheeses, meats and other delicious Nova Scotia products at Pier 20 six days a week.

Harbour Ferry
A ferry ride across Halifax Harbour to Dartmouth provides some of the best photo opportunities of both the harbour and city.

Fisherman's Cove
A working fishing village in the Eastern Passage is an all-inclusive destination with art galleries, boutique shops and eateries as well as a small marine interpretive centre.

Full sail Spectators line the waterfront for the historic Parade of Sail that caps off the Tall Ships Festival, an event that Halifax has hosted several times in the past two decades.

Crystal glass and bronze This lens from the Sambro Island lighthouse, now displayed at the Maritime Museum, once lit the entrance to Halifax Harbour.

The Titanic Connection

The city will always be linked to the sinking of the RMS *Titanic* for the role it played in the aftermath of the tragedy. As the closest port with direct rail and steamship connections, rescue ships brought the bodies here to be shipped home. Victims were buried at three city cemeteries, including the Fairview Lawn Cemetery, where the graves of the "unknown child" and J. Dawson—thanks to the 1998 movie *Titanic*—attract the curious.

The Maritime Museum of the Atlantic has an impressive exhibit on the *Titanic*. It is also the place to tour the hydrographic vessel the CSS *Acadia*, a well-preserved Edwardian ocean steamship, as well as to learn about shipbuilding, shipwrecks and another great marine disaster, the Halifax Explosion of 1917. The collision of a munitions ship with another warship resulted in an explosion that killed 1,950 people and injured thousands; it also destroyed much of the city.

Around Nova Scotia

Fort Anne The Officers' Quarters served as the barracks for officers and soldiers until the withdrawal of the garrison from Fort Anne in 1854.

WOLFVILLE

The pretty university town of Wolfville has shady tree-lined streets and grand Victorian homes reminiscent of New England, a nod to the wave of New Englanders who arrived after the American Revolution. Although closely entwined with its Acadian past, it also has a vibrant cultural community with theatre companies and art galleries showcasing the work of island artists, including local resident Alex Colville, one of the province's best-known artists. Centuries-old dikes constructed by the Acadians to divert salt water to irrigate land can be viewed from Waterfront Park by bike and foot along the dikes, including a trail linking Wolfville and Grand Pré. The Grand Pré National Historic Site, located on the original Acadian settlement, commemorates the Grand Deportation of the Acadians by the British in 1755. A statue of Evangeline, the young Acadian heroine immortalized in Henry Wadsworth Longfellow's epic poem, and a memorial church and gardens grace the site. Near Grand Pré, Evangeline Beach attracts thousands of sandpipers and plovers each summer, who stop to feed on the Minas Basin mud flats. This basin also has some of the highest tides in the Bay of Fundy.

PLANNING

Visit in late summer when migrating birds travel the Atlantic Flyway. Wolfville's arts scene entertains throughout the year.

🌲 🏛 🐦 ✈

ANNAPOLIS ROYAL

The story of Annapolis Royal, the first capital of the Colony of Nova Scotia, begins nearby at the Port-Royal National Historic Site of Canada, an early 17th-century reconstruction

of Habitation at Port-Royal, the original French settlement that began as a fur trading post in 1605 at the mouth of the Annapolis River.

Annapolis Royal's saga continues at the Fort Anne National Historic Site, where some of the original buildings, including a late-18th-century British officers' quarters and powder magazine, have been restored. Built in the early 18th century by the French to protect the town against attacks from the sea, the star-shaped fort was renamed Fort Anne when the British gained control.

The 4-hectare Annapolis Royal Historic Gardens represent four centuries of horticultural history in the province from the sustainable Acadian vegetable and herb garden to more elaborate Victorian and rose gardens.

PLANNING
Annapolis is best visited in summer or early autumn; most of the attractions are closed from November through April.

🌲 👫 🏛 🏛

Bras d'Or Lake Sailboats pass the Kidston Island lighthouse, established in 1875 to aid traffic on Bras d'Or Lake, which, despite its name, is an inland sea.

BADDECK
Inventor Alexander Graham Bell made Baddeck, a picturesque resort community on the Bras d'Or Lake on Cape Breton Island, his home for many years. After his death, his daughters donated many of his inventions and possessions to Canada with the stipulation that they remain in Baddeck. In 1956 the Alexander Graham Bell Museum opened, featuring exhibits on his work with the deaf, his aviation and hydrofoil experiments, and his numerous inventions, as well as his family life. The *Elsie*, a sleek 55-foot yacht designed by Bell for sailing on the Bras d'Or Lake, sails daily in summer from the Inverary Resort marina, cruising by Beinn Bhreagh Hall, Bell's summer estate, as well as nesting sites of bald eagles. Nightly ceilidhs offer lively performances at the Saltwater Theatre. The internationally acclaimed Celtic Colours Festival is held at various locations throughout Cape Breton, including Baddeck, in early October.

PLANNING
While summer is best for water sports, the fun continues into autumn with festivals and ceilidhs drawing crowds.

🌲 👫 🏛 🐦 🐟 🐋

Forging iron Visitors are whisked back to fortress life at Louisbourg in 1744 with the help of "residents" in period dress.

LOUISBOURG
The biggest attraction at Louisbourg, which lies on the remote eastern shores of Cape Breton Island, is its fortress. Founded in 1713 by the French to protect their fishing grounds and defend the St. Lawrence River against enemy attack, Louisbourg Fortress was captured twice, first in 1745 by New Englanders and regained through treaty, and then 13 years later by the British, who eventually abandoned it. In 1960 reconstruction of the original walled fortress began. The 5-hectare site is the largest historical reconstruction in North America, with more than 50 historically accurate reconstructed buildings, among them the captain's house, artillery storehouses and the king's bastion—a fortress within the fort. The town also has an interesting railway museum and a 17th-century-style playhouse offering live theatre and concerts featuring Cape Breton music.

PLANNING
For the whole experience at the fortress, plan a full-day visit from June through September.

👫 🏛

CAPE CHIGNECTO

With its dramatic seascapes, unusual geological features and 29 kilometres of pristine shoreline along the Bay of Fundy, Cape Chignecto Provincial Park is a jewel in Nova Scotia's park system. The 42-square-kilometre wilderness park accommodates day hikers and backpackers with an extensive trail system that traverses deep valleys, old growth forest and beach areas and yields breathtaking views of the water. Cliffs 185 metres high pierce the sky as they rise majestically from the Bay of Fundy, which is heralded for having the highest tides in the world. Trails cut through old logging camps and ghost towns, such as Eatonville, which is accessible through a day-use area on the northern end of the park. From there it's a short walk to Seal Cove, where the Three Sisters, a trio of red-rock sea stacks, guard the bay, and to the raised beach at Squally Point, another geological wonder.

PLANNING

Although the park closes from November to May, other areas on the cape provide good cross-country skiing throughout the winter.

🌲 👪 🏛 🛷 🎿 ⛵

PICTOU

The *Hector*, a three-masted wooden sailing ship, arrived on the Northumberland Shore in 1773 from Lochbroom, Scotland, bringing with it 33 families and 25 single men eager to start new lives in Nova Scotia, or "New Scotland." They settled in a natural harbour in what is now Pictou, turning to the sea for their livelihood and to feed their families, an industry that continues to this day. The story of their arduous two-and-a-half year journey is told at Harbour Heritage Quay. The 3-kilometre Jitney Walking Trail follows

Spectacular sea stacks The relentless pounding of waves in the Bay of Fundy have eroded the headland, isolating big chunks of rock known as sea stacks.

Full-scale model A walk-aboard replica of the *Hector* can be found at Harbour Heritage Quay in Pictou, along with a blacksmith's forge and carpentry shop.

the waterfront to the landing site of the *Hector*. The Northumberland Fisheries Museum offers an insightful look at the local fishing heritage, including a vintage lobster boat, authentic fisherman's bunkhouse and cannery exhibit. Rare live lobsters, including a blue lobster, are on display.

PLANNING
Visit in July for the Pictou Lobster Carnival, first held in 1934, and one of Nova Scotia's signature events. August brings the annual Hector Festival.
🕴️ 🏛️ 🐟

YARMOUTH

While some speculate that Norse explorer Leif Ericson once came ashore at what is now Yarmouth, hard evidence that French explorer Samuel de Champlain made landfall in 1604 comes from Cape Forchu. He named the peninsula of land jutting into the Gulf of Maine, "forked tongue of land." Cape Forchu Lightstation, the second-most photographed lighthouse in Nova Scotia after Peggy's Cove, stands at the tip of the cape. The light keeper's house is now a museum about the lighthouse and the men and their families who kept the light operating for more than a century. The original French fishing settlement quickly grew into a prosperous wooden shipbuilding centre and later a major port for commercial fishing and steamships travelling between Nova Scotia and New England. The Yarmouth County Museum and Archives documents the town's long seafaring and fisheries history, as does the W. Laurence Sweeney Fisheries Museum. This interactive museum recreates Yarmouth's waterfront of yesteryear and the everyday operations of the now-defunct Sweeney Fisheries, with items preserved from when the company closed its doors. The Firefighters' Museum of Nova Scotia chronicles the history of firefighting in the province and has one of the oldest surviving steam-powered fire engines in Canada.

PLANNING
Visit in July, August and September for Musique de la Baie, nightly "kitchen parties," an Acadian tradition, featuring local musicians, songs and stories.
🕴️ 🏛️

SHELBURNE

An inviting coastal town on what is one of the finest natural harbours in the world, Shelburne celebrates a diverse cultural history extending from the early encampments of the native Mi'kmaq

through the arrival of Loyalists in the 1780s after the American Revolutionary War. As the population swelled, so did the area's economy, which centred on fishing and shipbuilding. The waterfront heritage district features a number of buildings dating back to Loyalist times, which made it an ideal location for the 1994 movie *The Scarlet Letter*. The cluster of museums that comprise the Shelburne Historic Complex provides a window into the Loyalist history of eastern Canada, beginning with the Shelburne County Museum's collections. On the lane behind the museum, the Ross Thomson House, built in 1784–85 by Scottish brothers George and Robert Ross, combines a general store and living quarters, restored as it was in the 1820s. The J. C. Williams Dory Shop on the waterfront has a collection of fishing dories and a boat-building workshop. Maritime crafts of all types are on view at the Muir-Cox Shipyard Museum and Shipbuilding Interpretive Centre.

PLANNING
Go in September to experience Shelburne's quirkier side, the Whirligig and Weathervane Festival, which showcases regional folk art.
🕴️ 🏛️ 🖼️

Cape Forchu Lightstation The beam from the 23-metre-high lighthouse is visible to ships 30 nautical miles away.

THE CABOT TRAIL

The Cabot Trail meanders for almost 300 kilometres through Cape Breton Island, one of the most spectacular parts of Nova Scotia, with one third of its route traversing Cape Breton Highlands National Park. Winding through rugged coastal headlands and craggy highlands, it connects several small communities and different cultures from Scottish and Irish to Acadian French. If the stunning vistas are not enough, it's rife with festivals, music and places to hike, kayak and observe whales and other wildlife.

Planning:
Setting aside at least a day, preferably two or three, to drive the loop in any season, allows ample time to stop and explore.

Around Prince Edward Island

CHARLOTTETOWN

Situated on a harbour at the confluence of the Hillsborough River and its tributaries, Charlottetown is a blend of old and new. Although the smallest of Canada's provincial capitals, it is considered the birthplace of Canada. It was here that the famous Articles of Confederation were drawn up at the Charlottetown Conference of 1864 to form a new country, the Dominion of Canada. The annual Festival of the Fathers commemorates the event with a re-enactment of the landing of the Fathers of Confederation at Peake's Wharf and a march to Province House National Historic Site, where the conference took place. Province House has been the home of PEI's provincial legislature since 1847. At Founder's Hall, Canada's Birthplace Pavilion, visitors relive Canadian history. The restored Historic Charlottetown Waterfront helps tell the town's story by capturing the essence of an earlier era, when shipbuilding dominated the waterfront and wharves were bustling with trade ships, such as schooners carrying timber to Europe. The Confederation Centre of the Arts, built as a monument to the Fathers of the Confederation, is dedicated to the visual and performing arts.

PLANNING

With most attractions open year-round, winter or spring means fewer crowds. For Peake's Wharf's summer concert series and the Festival of the Fathers, visit in summer.

CAVENDISH

Cavendish, known as the home of the little orphan Anne Shirley from the novel *Anne of Green Gables*, sits on PEI's northern shores at the western entrance to Prince Edward Island National Park. The Green Gables House, a National Historic Site of Canada since 1937, is open for tours, as is the author's birthplace in New London, 11 kilometres southwest of Cavendish. Anne fans will also want to visit Avonlea Village, a theme park based on *Anne of Green Gables*.

PLANNING

Anne's house is open for tours only from May through October.

VICTORIA-BY-THE-SEA

Laidback Victoria-by-the-Sea is the place for biking, digging clams or to watch boats. Once a bustling commercial seaport thanks to its sheltered harbour and key location on the Northumberland Strait, today, in quiet contrast, Victoria-by-the-Sea has just a few antique shops and art galleries and a chocolate shop. The town's history can be explored at the Victoria Seaport Museum, in Palmer's Range Light. The Victoria Playhouse celebrates the town and island's heritage each summer with "Follow the Fiddler," a theatre pageant where the audience walks through town with the performers.

PLANNING
Visit in summer to catch performances of the Playhouse's summer season.
🚻 🏛 ⛵ 🖼

Quaint fishing village Victoria-by-the-Sea offers the perfect setting to sit back and relax, perhaps while watching the lobster boats bring in their catch.

Eastern Lighthouses

PEI's eastern shores are dotted with lighthouses from East Point to Point Prim. The oldest, Point Prim (right), was built in 1845 and is one of only two round brick lighthouses in the country. Panmure Island and Souris East Lighthouse offer panoramic 360-degree vistas from their lanterns. Woods Island Lighthouse's interpretive centre explores the area's seafaring history from shipwrecks to rum-running and fisheries. Cape Bear Lighthouse found fame as the first place in Canada to receive the distress signal from the sinking RMS *Titanic*.

SUMMERSIDE

Once a sleepy coastal town favoured by islanders for their own summer retreats, Summerside on Bedeque Bay has grown in size to be PEI's second largest city, but without sacrificing its maritime charm. Visitors can explore its boat-building and fishing heritage at Spinnakers' Landing on the Summerside Waterfront. Summer brings the annual lobster festival and the College of Piping's Celtic heritage celebration, which kicks off with the Summerside Highland Gathering and features ceilidhs and concerts throughout the summer. Murals depicting historical events grace many of its buildings; museums are dedicated to local history and former livelihoods including fox farming. The Eptek Arts and Culture Centre provides a year-round venue for island artists to display their work alongside its permanent collection of landscape paintings by the late Dr. Georgie Read Barton, a Summerside native.

PLANNING
A packed schedule of events that includes fun festivals and celebrations of PEI's Celtic heritage make summer the best time to visit.
🏛 ⛵ 🖼

A Dozen Great Beaches in Atlantic Canada

Cavendish Beach, Prince Edward Island

Set against a dramatic backdrop of red sandstone cliffs and marram grass-topped sand dunes, Cavendish Beach stretches for 8 kilometres along the Gulf of St. Lawrence, from New London Bay to Cavendish East. It's located in the 22-square-kilometre Prince Edward Island National Park, within walking distance of Green Gables, the house that author Lucy Maud Montgomery made famous through her tales of a little orphan girl named Anne.

The soft sand beach is a favourite of sunbathers and beach walkers as well as swimmers, particularly in the peak summer months of July and August, when the water, warmed by the Gulf Stream, averages between

15 and 20 degrees Celsius. Visitors can follow the Cavendish Dunelands Trail from the main beach area to Cavendish East, crossing over MacNeill's Pond on a floating boardwalk.

Signage along the trail describes the area's many natural, cultural and historical features. Canada geese and other waterfowl frequent the pond, while great blue herons often can be spotted wading in the marshes. Birdwatchers will find binoculars handy for scanning the towering beach cliffs for double-crested cormorants and black guillemots or for investigating the quieter stretches of sand for the endangered piping plover, which nests here in spring and summer. The national park has a

Other Great Beaches

Kelly's Beach, New Brunswick. Protected by a natural sandbar, the 6-kilometre-long beach in Kouchibouguac National Park can be accessed by boardwalk through salt marshes and Acadian forest and is home to a colony of grey seals.

New River Beach, New Brunswick. This pretty saltwater beach on the Fundy Coast is a favourite spot for beachcombers searching for sand dollars, starfish and sea glass.

Parlee Beach, New Brunswick. Found in Shediac on the Northumberland Strait, this swimming area is both one of the warmest saltwater beaches and most popular beaches in Atlantic Canada.

Cape Ray Beach, Newfoundland and Labrador. Located in J.T. Cheeseman Provincial Park, this beach is one of the best in the region for finding sea urchins, surf clams and other marine life.

Northern Bay Sands, Newfoundland and Labrador. A favourite with local families, this pristine, dark sand beach on Avalon Peninsula's Conception Bay stretches for 1 kilometre.

Sandy Cove Beach, Newfoundland and Labrador. Considered one of the finest natural sand beaches in Newfoundland and Labrador, its annual Celtic Folk Festival, featuring provincial and Irish music, is a big draw for both travellers and residents.

Ingonish Beach, Nova Scotia. Separated by a barachois—a sandbar between a coastal lake and the Atlantic Ocean—this Cape Breton Island beach offers both fresh and saltwater swimming.

Martinique Beach, Nova Scotia. The longest, white sand beach in Nova Scotia, the 5-kilometre Martinique Beach, in addition to being a favourite with surfers and swimmers, is a designated bird sanctuary and protected area for the piping plover.

Melmerby Beach, Nova Scotia. One of Nova Scotia's busiest beaches for swimming and digging clams, it is named for a ship that sank off its sandy shores in October 1890 en route to Quebec City.

Rissers Beach, Nova Scotia. This white sand beach, fringed by evergreen trees and grassy sand dunes, is a child-friendly spot that is popular for sandcastle competitions.

Basin Head Beach, Prince Edward Island. This sparkly sand beach in Basin Head Provincial Park, nicknamed the Singing Sands Beach, "sings," or squeaks, when walked on, a phenomenon that even scientists can't completely explain.

full-service campground, where visitors can camp near the beach. Plenty of activities are available in the area from horseback riding to golfing, sea kayaking, parasailing and deep sea fishing. Visitors may also go antiquing in one of the nearby fishing villages or farming communities.

Planning: Cavendish Beach is located on the island's north-central shore. The most publicly accessible area of the beach, where parking facilities, a snack bar, washrooms and changing rooms can be found, is near the end of Graham's Lane. Visit the nearby town of Cavendish in July for the multi-day Cavendish Beach Music Festival, featuring country music.

Discover New Brunswick

SAINT JOHN

New Brunswick's largest city, Saint John has an interesting mélange of cultures. Founded by the French and built by British Loyalists who fled the American Revolution, its deep-water harbour on the mouth of the Saint John River also attracted traders from faraway ports. Large numbers of Irish immigrants arrived in the mid-1800s when the Irish Potato Famine forced them from their homeland. The Irish influx changed the demographic, political and cultural landscape of this seaport city, which today has a lively arts scene and a multitude of flourishing businesses and restaurants. Its busy streets are a blend of different architectural styles, a hodgepodge of

Reversing Falls Twice daily the Bay of Fundy's mighty tides meet the Saint John River rapids, forcing the river to flow backward in a spectacular natural display.

wooden homes and red brick Victorians—many along King Street, the steepest, shortest street in Canada—huge stone churches and modern commerce buildings. Most were built after the Great Fire of 1877, although a few, including the 1823 neoclassical-style Old Courthouse and the Saint John City Market (see below), survived. The inferno levelled 80 hectares of the city, including more than 1,600 structures and several ships in the harbour.

The New Brunswick Museum, Canada's oldest continuously operating museum, chronicles the history of the province's industries, including wooden shipbuilding, along with exhibits on geology, wildlife, birds and art. Located in the downtown Market Square, a complex of hotels and restaurants, it's not far from Market Slip at the bottom of King Street, where Loyalists landed in 1783, or Barbour's General Store, a 19th-century reproduction of a country store with a post office and barber shop. The Carleton Martello Tower in West Saint John promises unsurpassed views of the city and the harbour. Now a National Historic Site, its exhibits and restored barracks and powder magazine help teach visitors about its role in the defence of the city that began with the War of 1812.

Saint John City Market

Occupying a full city block between Charlotte Street and Germain Street, the iconic Saint John City Market, with a ceiling like an inverted ship's keel, was built in 1876. As the oldest public market in North America, it is just as likely to be visited by prime ministers and movie stars as locals and visitors in the know. Stalls are filled with local fish, meats, preserves, dulse (dried seaweed) and produce. Vendors sell crafts and souvenirs, and eateries carry fresh lobster and other Atlantic Canada fare on their menus.

Fredericton With a river location, tree-lined avenues and well-preserved historic architecture reflecting its British past, Fredericton has an air of gentility about it.

Harbour Passage, an interconnected system of walking and biking trails, parks and heritage sites along the waterfront, provides water-level views of the working port and city, including Saint John's key attraction, the famous Reversing Falls. The tidal wave can be viewed from Irving Nature Park, a prime spot for sea kayaking and spotting whales, seals and seabirds. The 243-hectare park is an important stopover for shorebirds travelling the Atlantic Flyway between the Canadian Arctic and South America.

PLANNING
Museums, the Saint John City Market and many other attractions stay open throughout the year; summertime is busy.

♣ ⚺ 🏛 🖼 🐦 🛶

FREDERICTON
Considered the cultural, artistic and educational centre of New Brunswick, the province's capital, Fredericton, has a number of art galleries and museums as well as the oldest public university in North America. The Beaverbrook Art Gallery, which displays an impressive collection of 19th- and 20th-century works—including Salvador Dali's masterpiece, *Santiago el Grande*—is a legacy of newspaper magnate Lord Beaverbrook.

The city's Historic Garrison District on Queen Street, with its restored barracks, guardhouse and other buildings, provides a feel for life on a British post. The Fredericton Regional Museum is housed in the Officers' Quarters. The Old Government House and Provincial Legislature present another slice of New Brunswick's past as does the King's Landing Historical Settlement. The living history museum, 37 kilometres west of Fredericton, depicts everyday life in a typical, rural 19th-century New Brunswick village.

PLANNING
Don't miss the Harvest Jazz and Blues Festival, the east coast's largest celebration of jazz, blues and world music, in September.

⚺ 🏛 🖼

MOUNT CARLETON
Carved from a piece of remote wilderness in the north-central highlands of New Brunswick, the 174-square-kilometre Mount Carleton Provincial Park safeguards a landscape of pristine waterways, rare plant and animal species and mountain peaks

Mountain views A climb to the summit of any of Mount Carleton Provincial Park's peaks rewards hikers with dazzling views of colourful foliage in autumn.

formed from 400-million-year-old volcanic rock. The park's centrepiece is 820-metre Mount Carleton, the highest peak in the Maritime Provinces. The trail to its craggy summit ends with a superb 360-degree view of its lakes, the 562-metre Bailey Peak and other mountains in the park. A ridge walk connects Mount Sagamook and Carleton via Mount Head. More than 60 kilometres of trails afford opportunities for watching wildlife and for recreation. The park supports a diverse wildlife population, including lynx, white-tailed deer, black bear, bobcat and two rare rodents, the Gaspé shrew and the yellow-nosed rock vole. Moose are commonly sighted in the Nepisiguit Lakes region, a chain of three freshwater lakes popular with kayakers and canoeists. More than 150 species of birds have been recorded here, including Bicknell's thrush, found only in high elevations. Two rare plant species, alpine blueberry and Bigelow's sedge, cling to Mount Carleton's slopes.

PLANNING
This year-round outdoor playground is open to hikers, mountain bikers and boaters in the warmer months and cross-country skiers and snowmobilers in winter.

♣ ⚺ 🚲 🐦 🎿 ⛷

FUNDY

Although one of Canada's smallest national parks, Fundy National Park on the Bay of Fundy is among its best-known due to a big phenomenon: the highest tidal fluctuation in the world. The giant tides, which produce tidal shifts of up to 15 metres, cover the ocean bed twice daily, depositing seaweed and intertidal species as the tides slowly retreat. Over the centuries the tides created stunning coastal scenery, including sea caves and towering seaside cliffs, where the endangered peregrine falcon nests.

The 206-square-kilometre park, accessed from the village of Alma at its eastern end, is crisscrossed by more than 120 kilometres of hiking and mountain biking trails. The park preserves some of the last virgin stands of red spruce in eastern North America and harbours the documented world's oldest red spruce tree, a 400-year-old specimen. Wildlife sightings are common, including moose feeding in bogs and around the remote Marven Lake and Chambers Lake, red squirrels, snowshoe hares and white-tailed deer. Bennett Lake is best for water sports.

PLANNING

Peak season is late spring through autumn; trails provide options to snowshoe and ski in winter. Or stay overnight in an insulated yurt.

MONCTON

The first officially bilingual Canadian city, Moncton embraces its strong connection to Acadia through its museums, cultural centre and one of only two French-language universities in the Maritimes. Its proximity to the Acadian Coast, which stretches from Shediac north along New Brunswick's eastern seaboard, makes it the unofficial Gateway to Acadia. Both the Lutz Mountain Heritage Museum and the University of Moncton's Acadian Museum have impressive collections of artifacts reflecting 300 years of Acadian history. Acadia is also centre stage at the Aberdeen Cultural Centre, which houses several dance and theatre companies and art galleries, including one representing contemporary Acadian artists. Moncton is a river city, on the bend of the Petitcodiac River, known for its tidal bore—a natural phenomenon caused by the surging tides in the Bay of Fundy. The best viewing point is the aptly named Bore View Park, which connects to the Riverfront Promenade. Magnetic Hill, a gravity optical illusion, and Moncton's zoo, the largest in Atlantic Canada, are popular with visitors.

PLANNING
Moncton is nicely positioned as a base for exploring places as close as Hopewell Rocks or farther afield to the cities, towns and parks of New Brunswick.
††† 🏛 🏯

ACADIAN VILLAGE
At Village Historique Acadien, or Acadian Historic Village, located on New Brunswick's Acadian coast, men work the fields while the one-room schoolhouse resounds with the recitations of children and the women prepare a hearty noontime meal. Located near Caraquet, New Brunswick's oldest

Confederation Bridge

Celebrated as a marvel of engineering for its unique design, construction and safety features, Confederation Bridge opened to traffic in 1997, linking New Brunswick and Prince Edward Island. At its highest span, 60 metres above water, large ocean-going ships can slip between its massive steel piers, spaced 250 metres apart. While it's the world's longest bridge over ice-covered water and designed to last for a century, it is the superb views on the 12.9-kilometre drive that impress travellers the most.

History comes alive Dirt roads in Acadian Village wind past churches, dwellings with well-tended gardens, utilitarian farm buildings and trade shops.

Acadian community, the living history museum portrays the colourful culture, history and traditions of these proud people from the time of the deportations to the mid-20th century. Many of the more than 40 buildings are authentic Acadian structures moved here from throughout the province. In the village, bilingual interpreters go about their daily work, demonstrating spinning, bread baking, carpentry, blacksmithing and other skills. Hôtel Château Albert, a replica of a turn-of-the-last-century hotel that once existed in Caraquet, has been recreated at the village for overnight guests who want an authentic 1907 hotel experience. Staff dress in appropriate garb and modern amenities are few. The nearby Musée Acadien de Caraquet, in Caraquet, also provides insight into the French-speaking Acadian people.

PLANNING
While primarily a summer attraction, the Village Historique Acadien opens its grounds for walkers during its offseason at no charge.
††† 🏛

Miramichi With many rivers in the area providing some of the best fishing in the world, Miramichi has become synonymous with angling.

MIRAMICHI
Found in the upper reaches of the province, Miramichi is an outdoor paradise for anglers. The Miramichi Salmon Conservation Centre, Canada's oldest fish hatchery, is located here, as is the French Fort Cove Eco Centre, where visitors can learn about Atlantic salmon and wildlife, as well as an event that shook the city—the Great Miramichi Fire of 1825. The fire wiped out entire towns in the region as well as surrounding forests, leading to the demise of the ship mast making industry on the Miramichi River. Visitors can hear about the 19th-century shipbuilding industry on Beaubears Island. Boat tours to the Boishébert and Beaubears Island Shipbuilding National Historic Site of Canada leave from Ritchie Wharf. Music and oral histories at the Metepenagiag Heritage Park relate the history of the local First Nation people, the Mi'kmaq of Metepenagiag. The city also draws crowds for its many festivals, including the Miramichi Folksong Festival and Canada's Irish Festival on the Miramichi.

PLANNING
The Miramichi River's fly-fishing season for Atlantic salmon begins on April 15.
🌲 ††† 🏛 🪑 🛶 ⟿

Around the Fundy Isles

ST. ANDREWS

Located on Passamaquoddy Bay, the attractive seaside town of St. Andrews-By-The-Sea stands out for its historic architecture, including the stately century-old Fairmont Algonquin, a grand Tudor-style hotel. More than half of the town's buildings predate 1880, including the Old County Courthouse, County Gaol, the War of 1812 Blockhouse and Greenock Presbyterian Church, with 14 structures surviving from the 1700s. The Huntsman Marine Laboratory-Aquarium provides an introduction to the marine life and beach creatures of the region, while Kingsbrae Garden celebrates St. Andrews' horticultural heritage through 11 hectares of themed gardens. Nearby Ministers Island was once the summer home of Sir William Van Horne, who reportedly acquired the 200-hectare estate in 1890 in a poker game. The estate is accessible only at low tide by guided tour, which includes the 50-room mansion and outbuildings, among them a livestock barn that housed the wealthy railway mogul's creamery and stables for his thoroughbred horses and Dutch belted cattle.

PLANNING

Many of the guided tours and attractions are available only from early summer through Thanksgiving.

ST. STEPHEN

The border town of St. Stephen on the St. Croix River just across from Calais, Maine, is the gateway to Atlantic Canada. It enjoys a reputation as Canada's Chocolate Town, thanks to the entrepreneurial Gangong brothers, James and Gilbert, who introduced homemade chocolates to their line of grocery products in the late 1800s. The Chocolate Museum, located in the former Gangong Brothers factory building, commemorates the history of candy-making in St. Stephen with displays of antique equipment and decorative chocolate gift boxes and with demonstrations. The history of shipbuilding, lumbering and other local industries are chronicled at the Charlotte County Museum. Just outside town, outdoor enthusiasts can hike or go birdwatching at the 135-hectare Ganong Nature Park at Todd's Point.

PLANNING

Plan a visit to St. Stephen to coincide with the annual Chocolate Festival in midsummer, one of the biggest local events of the year.

GRAND MANAN

Roughly 10 kilometres from the mainland, Grand Manan, the Queen Mother of the Fundy Isles, was a favourite of naturalist John James Audubon and novelist Willa Cather. From North Head, where the mainland ferry from Black Harbour docks, to Southwest Head, a 32-kilometre road winds past somnolent seaside towns, ephemeral seascapes and vintage wooden lighthouses, including the 1860 Swallowtail Lighthouse. The Grand Manan Museum is housed in the former dwelling of Moses Gerrish, an original island settler. Among the quirkier stops are Hole-in-the-Wall, an unusual rock formation, and Roland's Sea Vegetables, where dulse, a type of seaweed, and other sea plants are sun-dried and packaged for sale. Grand Manan is the starting point for trips to Machias Seal Island, where the rare Atlantic puffin nests in the company of razorbill auks and Arctic terns. A limited number of visitors are allowed on the refuge daily in summer to observe and photograph these comical-looking birds.

Watching whales Boat excursions that get up close to majestic whales are popular in Grand Manan, as are tours of the Whale and Seabird Station.

Deer Island With most of the population relying on the sea for its livelihood, colourful fishing boats, lobster pounds and herring weirs dominate the townscapes.

PLANNING
Book a whale-watch in summer. More than 300 species of migrating birds stop on the island in spring and autumn.
🌲 🏛 🪑 🐦 ⛵

DEER ISLAND

Accessible from the mainland via a free car ferry from Letete near St. George, Deer Island has a picture postcard familiarity. Northern Harbour has the world's biggest lobster pound—a holding structure for lobsters prior to shipment—while scenic inlets vie with natural wonders, such as the Old Sow, the largest natural tidal whirlpool in North America, for the photographer's attention. The whirlpool can be viewed from Deer Island Point Park on the island's southern tip or by guided boat trips from the mainland.

PLANNING
The ferry offers year-round access; summer and autumn promise the best weather.
🌲 🪑 ⛵

CAMPOBELLO ISLAND

Once a popular summer retreat for the social elite, Campobello Island pays homage to its most famous seasonal resident, the U.S. president Franklin Delano Roosevelt, with a 1,130-hectare park that's jointly managed by Canada and the United States. The small museum and visitor centre at Roosevelt Campobello International Park provide glimpses into Roosevelt's life on the island, but the real attraction is the summer home. This 34-room "cottage" appears frozen in time, as if the family had just left for a morning sail or picnic on the pebbly beach in what is now Herring Cove Provincial Park. About one third of the island is undeveloped, inviting visitors to wander through its forests and along its rock cliffs, beaches and bays.

PLANNING
Roosevelt's home is open only from Victoria Day through Thanksgiving.
🌲 👫 🏛 🪑

Beacon of light Head Harbour (East Quoddy Head) Lighthouse, built in 1829 and Canada's oldest wooden lighthouse, is on the northern tip of Campobello.

QUEBEC

Northern and Eastern Quebec

NUNAVIK REGION

Located north of the 55th parallel, Nunavik is a vast, remote land where caribou outnumber human inhabitants and isolated communities are accessible only by air. Considered Quebec's last frontier, its fragile natural beauty lies in an Arctic landscape of frozen tundra, taiga, boreal forests and countless lakes and bays. Its 11,000 people, mostly Inuits, live in 14 coastal communities along 2,500 kilometres of coastline on Hudson Bay, the Hudson Strait and Ungava Bay, where hunting, fishing and gathering to fill the community food storage locker is still part of everyday life. The experience and knowledge of the Inuits make them excellent outfitter guides for caribou hunts and fishing trips. The 507,000-square-kilometre territory's largest community is Kuujjuaq (Inuktitut for "big river"), which like many of the villages began as a fur-trading post. Situated 360 kilometres farther north, Inukjuak, where *Nanook of the North* was filmed in 1922, has a number of archaeological sites along the river. An impressive collection of Inuit arts and crafts, traditional tools and fishing and hunting gear can be viewed at the Daniel Weetaluktuk Museum. Bas-relief sculptures depicting daily life are on display at the Innalik School.

Just offshore, the Hopewell Islands are the summer nesting grounds for migratory birds including the barnacle goose. Beluga whales and seals are often spotted along Nunavik's coast. Caribou, musk ox, grey wolves and other large mammals are common on land. The Leaf River herd, the world's largest herd of migratory caribou, numbers more than 600,000 head. In summer, the animals often roam through the 1,134-square-kilometre Parc national des Pingualuit. Nunavik's first national park, it was created to protect the 267-metre-deep Pingualuk Lake formed by a 1.3-million-year-old meteor crater. The nearest village is Kangiqsujuaq, 88 kilometres away, but a flight to Lac Laflamme takes you to within a 45-minute trek to the crater. Nunavik's other national park, Parc national Kuururjuaq near Kangiqsualujjuaq, offers wilderness hiking, camping, backcountry skiing and river expeditions, all centred near the 160-kilometre Koroc River, which flows from the Torngat Mountains to Ungava Bay.

PLANNING

Summer has the nicest weather but late spring is best for observing migrating birds and August through May for the aurora borealis, or northern lights.

Snow route Snowmobiles may not be traditional, but they are ideal for the Inuits as they travel through snow-covered Nunavik in winter.

Weather-carved limestone There are more monoliths, or sea stacks, concentrated in Mingan Archipelago than in any other region in Canada.

LACS-ALBANEL-MISTASSINI-ET-WACONICHI

With its cold, deep waters teeming with walleye, northern pike, lake trout and speckled trout, Lac Mistassini, Quebec's largest natural freshwater lake, is an angler's paradise. It's among thousands of lakes and rivers within the boundaries of Réserve faunique des Lacs-Albanel-Mistassini-et-Waconichi in Quebec's mid-north wilderness region, many ideal for angling or canoe-camping. The French established a trading post on the 176-kilometre-long Lac Mistassini in 1672 to trade for furs with the native peoples. Large populations of beavers, otters and mink still thrive in these waters along with waterfowl, including common loons and common mergansers. The open forests, dominated by black spruce and other boreal species, harbour more than 30 species of animals, among them wolves, red foxes and martens. More than 100 bird species have been spotted on the 16,400-square-kilometre wilderness reserve, including bald eagles, great horned owls and other birds of prey.

PLANNING

The fishing season extends for three months beginning around June 1. Wild mushrooms and berries can be harvested in September.

MINGAN

Accessible only by boat, the string of 40 limestone islands that comprise the Mingan Archipelago are flush with unusual geological formations, rare plant species, seabirds and seals. The diverse ecosystems found in this national park reserve in the Gulf of St. Lawrence support an amazing number of mammal species and more than 200 species of birds, including Atlantic puffins, black guillemots, double-crested cormorants and many woodland warblers. Nearly 100 of its 450 plant species are rare or endangered and include numerous Arctic-alpine plants that generally do not survive this far south. The archipelago's most unusual feature is its dramatic topography including its stratified limestone sea stacks, sculpted by waves, wind and harsh weather. The elements have also carved away rock to form sea cliffs, arches and grottoes, many of which can be viewed by guided boat tour, sea kayak or shoreline walk.

Iconic Porcé Rock Accessible on foot at low tide from the town of Percé, this massive monolith is one of the largest natural arches in the world.

PLANNING

Marine transportation to the islands is available only from June to early September; reservations are advised. Overnight camping is allowed on some islands by permit only.

L'ÎLE-BONAVENTURE-ET-DU-ROCHER-PERCÉ

The cacophony of cries from the colony of northern gannets on Bonaventure Island builds to a crescendo as the more than 60,000 breeding pairs call to their mates. The world's largest and most accessible nesting site of this seabird, the sanctuary (also home to guillemots, black-legged kittiwakes and Atlantic puffins) is part of Parc national de l'Île-Bonaventure-et-du-Rocher-Percé. Tour boats make the 75-minute trip to Bonaventure Island, where four trails, a total of 15 kilometres, culminate at the noisy gannet colony at the island's eastern end. Sentier chemin-du-roy, the longest trail, provides the best ocean views. Visitors can explore a handful of 19th-century fishermen's houses near the dock.

PLANNING

Boat and island tours to Bonaventure are offered only May through October, when the gannets are nesting.

PARC NATIONAL DU BIC

Parc national du Bic, a rugged coastal park in the St. Lawrence maritime estuary near Rimouski, is defined by its unusual topography. Over the centuries, wind, surf and glacial activity have carved up its coastline, creating deep inlets and bays, islands, raised beaches, tombolos and towering cliffs, many home to botanical rarities. The common eider and other marine bird species nest in the rocky cliffs, while the park's beaches and reefs are a playground for common and grey seals in summer. At low tide seals can be seen at Sectors Cap-Caribou and Anse-aux-Bouleaux Ouest. Sector Pointe-aux-Épinettes and l'Anse des Pilotes, reached by a short trail, provide the best viewing at other times. Sightings of bald eagles and raptors, particularly during their autumn migration, are common from Saint-Fabien-sur-Mer at the western end of the park. A 25-kilometre network of trails yields panoramic views of the 33-square-kilometre park. In winter, hiking trails become cross-country ski and snowshoe trails.

Wildflower display Purple irises grow near a boulder-lined shore in Parc national du Bic.

PLANNING
Visit in winter to build an igloo, in autumn to hike the trails and in summer to spot wildlife.

LE JARDIN DES GLACIERS

A journey through Le Jardin des glaciers near Baie-Comeau reveals a wondrous tale of nature from a time when the Laurentide Ice Sheet, the world's largest glacier, covered this region of Quebec. The three-part attraction, which is centred in the Manicouagan-Uapishka region, a designated UNESCO World Biosphere Reserve, explores the last ice age, global climate change and the migration of the earliest peoples. At the Glacier Exploration Station a multimedia experience takes visitors deep into a glacier to look at climate change. The Maritime Adventure Park focuses on nature, with guided treks to Seashell Valley to explore a glacial delta and huge seashell deposit, and a boat tour on the St. Lawrence River to observe massive furrows, carved canyons, inlets, moraines and other glacial evidence. An easy walking trail links recreated dwellings of ice age

Natural climber A lone, sure-footed caribou manoeuvres the rugged terrain above the clouds in Parc national de la Gaspésie.

people for an understanding of how they lived. A visit to the Cyber Centre ties together all the information.

PLANNING
Plan on two days to explore all the attraction, open June to mid-October, has to offer.

PARC DE LA GASPÉSIE

A mosaic of boreal and subalpine forests, glacial lakes and treeless tundra, Parc national de la Gaspésie lies in the Gaspé Peninsula's rugged interior. Réserve faunique des Chic-Chocs flanks its eastern

Museum with a view Built in 1914 as an academy for boys, Musée acadien du Québec overlooks pretty Chaleur Bay.

end with another wildlife reserve, Réserve faunique de Matane, tucked against its western border. The 802-square-kilometre park includes 25 of the 40 highest mountain peaks in the province, including 1,268-metre Mont Jacques-Cartier and 1,154-metre Mont-Albert in the Chic-Chocs range. The only herd of woodland caribou in southern Quebec can often be observed feeding on lichen and mosses on the alpine slopes. The mountain microclimate is also ideal for Arctic mountain avens, starry saxifrage and more than a few dozen other Arctic-alpine plants. Moose are abundant as are white-tailed deer, coyotes and red fox. The park's geological and botanical diversity, vast tracts of untouched land and extensive network of backcountry trails, including one that traverses the entire width of the park, make this the perfect destination for hiking, snowshoeing, cross-country skiing and birdwatching. Several day hikes start from the Lac Cascapédia area, which is also a popular spot for canoeing.

PLANNING

Although open year-round, not all park services are available every season.

🌲 👫 🛷 🐦 🎿 🛶 🦅

BONAVENTURE

Tricolored Acadian flags, hung with pride, wave from homes and buildings throughout Bonaventure, a picturesque seaside town on Chaleur Bay. Although this well-protected harbour was an attractive port for traders and sea captains, it wasn't until 1760 that the area was permanently settled. A group of Acadians, who avoided deportation by the British, chose this location for their new home. Their story is told at the Musée acadien du Québec, which also houses a display of the town in miniature showcasing its Acadian and maritime heritage. On-site craft shops feature the work of local artisans.

At Bonaventure's Bioparc a 1.6-kilometre path connects five ecosystems—bay, lagoon, river, forest and tundra—found in the Gaspé region, with each one showcasing its native animal and plant species. Visitors can learn about the area's geology at Parc national de Miguasha, an important fossil site, which is also located on Chaleur Bay.

The warm saltwater beach and crystal-clear Bonaventure River lend themselves to kayaking, fly-fishing for salmon and other aquatic outdoor recreation. Birdwatchers find the coastal areas, sheltered coastal lagoons, woods and river delta good for spotting a diverse number of woodland and seabirds.

PLANNING

Although the museum is open year-round, the Bioparc can only be explored from June through October.

🌲 👫 🏛 🖼 🐦 🛶 🦅

ÎLES DE LA MADELEINE

The beauty of Îles de la Madeleine, an archipelago in the Gulf of St. Lawrence with a handful of inhabited islands, lies in its remoteness and natural assets. Its unspoiled seascapes with stretches of sea-sculpted cliffs, undulating sand dunes and pale sand beaches are dotted with homes painted a riot of colours, an Atlantic Canada tradition. Roads wind past wharves lined with lobster-fishing boats and traditional herring smokehouses and through communities where the architecture and hospitality reflect the islands' Acadian heritage.

Planning:
Three or four days provide enough time to explore the main islands, which are accessible by air and sea. Go in summer for the beaches or early March to see the "whitecoats," or baby harp seals, being born on the ice floes.

Charlevoix Region and Saguenay

BAIE-SAINT-PAUL

Although the internationally acclaimed Cirque du Soleil got its start in Baie-Saint-Paul, today the town is all about the visual arts. With its historic mansard-roofed homes—four-sided roofs that become steeper about halfway down—and narrow streets, it appears as if it were lifted from a painted canvas. One of the oldest towns in the province, its location on the banks of a meandering river in the scenic Gouffre Valley makes it a favourite of landscape artists including some of Quebec's best, among them Jean Paul Lemieux and Marc-Aurèle Fortin. The Centre d'Art Baie-Saint-Paul, nestled next to the town's main church, displays the work of more than 20 artists from the Charlevoix region. Visitors wishing to purchase original art will find a diverse selection at the art galleries and boutiques in the town's cultural quarter. The Musée d'art contemporain of Baie-Saint-Paul promotes the works of regional artists from 1920 to 1970, including the Group of Seven, an iconic group of Canadian landscape painters. Located in an ultramodern, award-winning building, the museum hosts the annual Symposium of Modern Art every August, inviting a dozen artists to work together to create art in front of an audience,

PLANNING

Go in autumn for Rêves d'automne, a ten-day celebration that features landscape artists and street art.

🏛 🛋 🖼

LA MALBAIE

Pure, fresh air and stunning scenery are among reasons cited for visiting La Malbaie, a tourism destination that harks back to the steamboat era, when affluent vacationers from Montreal, Toronto and New York City summered here. Former U.S. President William Howard Taft chose the area for a summer White House. Other Canadian and American politicians also considered this to be the ideal getaway.

Today, this tourist-friendly resort town has year-round appeal. Winter visitors can take advantage of fresh-packed powder at Mont Grand-Fonds, a family ski resort 14 kilometres from town. In summer everyone's attention turns to gardens, museums and outdoor recreation. At Centre écologique de Port-au-Saumon aquariums, touch tanks and guided walks introduce the Saguenay-St. Lawrence Marine Park ecosystem. The largest private garden in Canada, the 8-hectare Les Jardins des Quatre Vents, or Four Winds, is open to the public on select occasions, while Les Jardins du cap à l'Aigle is recognized for its impressive lilac collection. The Musée de Charlevoix features artifacts and artwork documenting the region's history and draw as an artists' colony. A guided tour of La Maison du Bootlegger, now a restaurant, reveals a labyrinth of secret passageways added during Prohibition to protect patrons visiting a hidden speakeasy. Visitors can also try their luck at a local casino.

PLANNING

Easy access to the popular Mont Grand-Fonds ski area makes winter a favourite time to visit. In summer, enjoy Le Domaine Forget, an international music festival.

🌲 👫 🏛 🖼 🎿

THE FLAVOUR TRAIL

A 143-kilometre self-drive route through one of Quebec's prettiest regions introduces visitors to the unique flavours of Charlevoix. Known as La Route des Saveurs, it includes more than two dozen food producers and a number of restaurants featuring locally produced foods on their menus. Most of the agricultural enterprises on this culinary circuit offer tastings and on-site sales of their products including cider, pâté de foie gras, duck, lamb and local produce in season. Artisanal chocolate shops and bakeries sell delicious sweet treats. The region is well-known for its sheep's and cow's milk cheeses, including cheddar, Gruyère and various soft cheeses. One stop on the trail, Laiterie Charlevoix, has a small economuseum that demonstrates the art of cheese making. La Ferme Éboulmontaise invites children into the sheep barn to meet the baby lambs. There's also a smokehouse for salmon and other fish and a number

of vineyards and cider houses that make alcoholic beverages from local fruit. The route winds through fertile farm fields and past towns with steepled churches and historic stone houses, mainly following Routes 138 and 381 through the region that cradles the St. Lawrence River.

PLANNING

The route can be sampled in a day, but to truly savour all it has to offer plan to spend at least three or four days in the area.
👫 ⛵

L'ANSE-SAINT-JEAN

Established as a mission in 1668, L'Anse-Saint-Jean didn't come into its own until discovered in the early 1800s by a group of lumber prospectors. Situated on the breathtaking Saguenay Fjord, this unspoiled village is the ideal base for fishing, kayaking, sailing and boat tours, including a popular whale-watching excursion to Sainte-Rose-du-Nord, a pretty village on the opposite shore. It's also close to the 284-square-kilometre Parc national du Fjord-du-Saguenay, a biologically diverse wilderness area with special appeal for hikers, kayakers and wildlife watchers. The park straddles the fjord, providing opportunities for kayak-camping along the banks. More than 100 kilometres of hiking trails offer panoramic views of the fjord and the St. Lawrence River. In winter the 23-kilometre Les Caps Trail, which connects Rivière-Éternité in the western end of the park and L'Anse-Saint-Jean on its eastern boundary, is a favourite with snowshoers and backcountry skiers. The three-day hike, with overnight accommodations in trail huts, traverses balsam fir and black spruce forests and mountain summits with superb vistas of the frozen fjord and snow-capped summits.

PLANNING

Plan on two to three days for kayaking or boat trips on the fjord, longer if hiking in the national park.
🌲 👫 ⛵ 🦆 🛶 🏔 🛥 🐦

Kayakers haven L'Anse-Saint-Jean, with the St. Lawrence River and fjord on its doorstep, is the ideal spot for water-sports enthusiasts.

SAGUENAY-ST. LAWRENCE

Belugas and harbour seals frolic in the cold, deep waters as seabirds soar overhead in Saguenay-St. Lawrence Marine Park, Quebec's first marine conservation park. Covering a 1,245-square-kilometre area, the park protects Saguenay Fjord and the northern portion of the St. Lawrence Estuary, the world's largest. Much of the action takes place on the water—kayaking, canoeing and scenic boat trips to enjoy the striking scenery and wildlife, especially whales. However, the park also accommodates scuba divers who want to explore the underwater marine life. Many of the park's 13 whale species, including the beluga, its only year-round resident, can also be observed from land at Cap-de-Bon-Désir. The Petit-Saguenay wharf offers the best view of the fjord, the longest in eastern Canada. The Marine Environment Discovery Centre in Haute-Côte-Nord, one of several park interpretive

centres, educates visitors about the estuary and takes them on a virtual underwater dive with a cameraman-naturalist. Many marine mammals and birds can be viewed from the cliff-top Pointe-Noire Interpretation and Observation Centre, located at the confluence of the estuary and the fjord. In La Baie at the park's western end, the Musée du Fjord explores the fjord's relationship with neighbouring communities.

PLANNING

Whales are most often spotted from May to October; most of the interpretive sites are open then.

🚶 👫 🏛 🛷 🦅 🐦 🛶 🐋

TADOUSSAC

Overlooking the estuary where the Saguenay River meets the St. Lawrence River, tiny Tadoussac is a big destination for observing whales, such as minke, fin, blue whales and

belugas. The Centre d'interprétation des mammifères marins features exhibits on whales, providing a good orientation before a whale-watch with a local tour company. Whales, along with seals and harbour porpoises, are also often observed from the free ferry that crosses the river to Baie-Sainte-Catherine. On land whale-watching is a popular activity at Pointe de l'Islet, a short distance from the wharf. A 30-minute walk up the hill yields panoramic vistas of the water and village. The 42-kilometre Sentier du Fjord affords magnificent views of the Saguenay Fjord on a three-day trek along its rocky shores. Tadoussac also enjoys the honour of being the site of the first fur-trading post in Canada, established in 1600. Visitors can explore a recreation of the post or seek out the Petite chapelle de Tadoussac, the oldest

Zoo Sauvage de Saint-Félicien

The Zoo sauvage de Saint-Félicien invites visitors into the natural habitats of native animal species that roam freely in expansive enclosures. Its "Sleeping with the Caribou" program is a full immersion into the animals' world that includes a "behind-the-scenes" zoo tour, visit to the animal nursery and an overnight stay in a prospector's tent in the middle of caribou habitat. Guests will have a chance to canoe on the lake, go moose tracking and learn about the boreal environment with dinner cooked over a campfire. They can also expect nocturnal visits from caribou, and sometimes moose and other creatures.

wooden church in Canada. Built in 1747, it contains a museum with period artifacts.

PLANNING
August and September are the peak months to see the most whale species.
🚣 🏛 ⛵ 🛶

GRANDS-JARDINS

Long considered an angler's paradise for its more than 60 fish-rich lakes swarming with speckled trout and Arctic char, Parc national

Ecclesial treasure Located near the Hotel Tadoussac, Petite Chapelle de Tadoussac was built by Jesuit missionaries to convert the local people to Christianity.

des Grands-Jardins protects a wilderness landscape of sparsely forested taiga and steep mountains. It was called the "Big Gardens" for its varied vegetation, including stands of dwarf birch, black spruce and sub-Arctic wildflowers. Carpets of lichens, not usually found this far south, support herds of woodland caribou. In autumn foliage season wild blueberries, mountain cranberries and black crowberries bathe the mountain slopes in reds and oranges. The hiking trail to the summit of the 980-metre-high Mont du Lac des Cygnes provides sublime views of the St. Lawrence River and the Charlevoix crater, formed when a large meteor hit the earth 350 million years ago. Other trails in the 30-kilometre network cross moose, wolf, lynx and deer habitat. The calm waters of Lac Turgeon and Lac Arthabaska are ideal for canoeing, while Rivière-Malbaie is best explored on a multi-day canoe-camping trip.

PLANNING
The 310-square-kilometre park, accessed through the village of Saint-Urbain, is well-suited for backcountry skiing and snowshoeing given its annual snowfall. Ice fishing is permitted on some of its lakes.
🎿 ⛷ 🦅 ❄ 🛶 🎣

L'ISLE-AUX-COUDRES

Accessible only by ferry from Saint-Joseph-de-la-Rive on the mainland, L'Isle-aux-Coudres has a proud maritime history extending back to 1535, when explorer Jacques Cartier first stepped foot on its shores. For centuries it was a secure anchorage for ships making the transatlantic crossing. In more recent times sea kayakers and canoeists have discovered its many bays and inlets. Musée les Voitures d'Eau tells the story of the island's boat-

Working mill The restored windmill at Les Moulins de l'Isle-aux-Coudres, which is on the Heritage Trail, a popular bike route, is still operational.

building industry, with displays of nautical equipment, vintage photos and a climb-aboard schooner, the *Mont-Saint-Louis*. The 11-kilometre island is best appreciated by bike. Its 40 kilometres of biking paths includes the 23-kilometre Heritage Trail that skirts the island's perimeter, encouraging cyclists to enjoy the views of the Gulf of St. Lawrence, sample fruit wines and ciders at Cidrerie et Verger Pedneault, or browse the art galleries and shops in Saint-Bernard, La Baleine and Saint-Louis. The bike trail also goes by Les Moulins de l'Isle-aux-Coudres, a flour-milling economuseum. The island parties in winter when it hosts a month-long winter carnival and a canoe race across the gulf. Trails also are open for snowmobilers and cross-country skiers.

PLANNING
Summer is best for biking and water sports, winter for Carnaval de Île-aux-Coudres.
🚣 🏛 ⛵ 📷 ⛷ 🛶

Exploring Quebec City

Resplendent with streetscapes lined with Parisian-style cafés, art galleries, museums and restored architecture, Quebec's fortified city radiates charm.

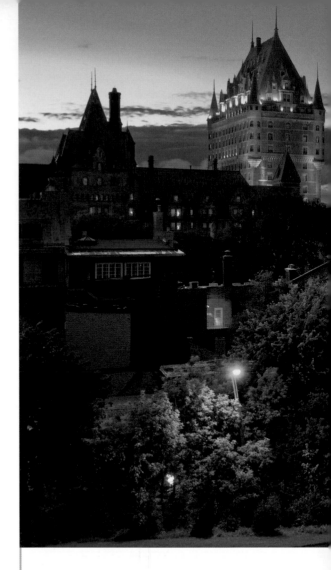

Illuminated skyline Designated a National Historic Site of Canada, Château Frontenac stands high above Quebec City's Lower Town and its port on the St. Lawrence River.

Quaint cobblestone streets wind past mansard-roofed buildings and colossal stone churches, while views from the bluffs of the St. Lawrence River produce gasps of awe. It's a place where history and culture meet and people linger over café au lait after an afternoon of shopping or strolling through the Vieux-Quebec, the city's oldest section. The city's architecture paints a picture of its complex history, of its beginnings as a fortified city, of its embracing of different religions and of its growth as a seat of government. Museums enlighten visitors to the city, which itself, in essence, is a big outdoor history museum. The largely francophone city also knows how to have a good time. Its population swells during Winter Carnival and a number of other great festivals.

Forts and Churches

Quebec City's European history begins with Samuel de Champlain, who built a fortress here in 1608. An interpretation centre at Place-Royale tells the story of this first habitation. Notre-Dame-des-Victoires, the province's oldest stone church, sits on the centuries-old square, now a favourite of street performers. Château St-Louis, Champlain's second fort, stood high on a cliff overlooking the St. Lawrence River near Château Frontenac, a massive castlelike hotel that dominates the skyline. Terrasse Dufferin, a boardwalk with incredible river and mountain views, extends from the hotel to the star-shaped La Citadelle, built to defend Quebec against America. It now stands guard over North America's only walled city.

Cultural Treasures

The city's reputation as a centre of arts and culture is well deserved. It has a world-class symphony orchestra, several performing arts venues and a profusion of art galleries. Its

Bird's-eye view Restaurants and other establishments in Quebec's old section combine European ambience with Québécois hospitality.

Don't Miss

Hôtel de Glace
Stop for a nightcap served in a glass made of ice or stay for the night to sleep on ice at North America's first ice hotel, open from early January through late March.

Wendake
Guided tours of the historic Wendake village on the edge of the downtown area provide insight into the history, traditions and culture of the Huron-Wendat Nation.

Quebec-Lévis Ferry
Some of the best views of the Quebec City skyline, including the Château Frontenac and Séminaire de Québec, can be had from the ferry boat that crosses the St. Lawrence River.

Saint-Roch District
This former industrial area has evolved into one of the city's trendiest districts for shopping, dining out and nightclubbing. It supports a number of artists' studios and galleries displaying contemporary works of local artists and artisans.

multitude of museums includes the Musée National des Beaux-Arts du Québec, which has one of the largest collections of Quebec art with large holdings of 17th-century and Inuit art. The core exhibits at the Musée de la civilisation de Québec focus on the people of Quebec, including the 11 aboriginal nations. Canada's oldest museum, the Musée de l'Amérique française, explores the development of French culture in North America. It occupies part of the Séminaire de Québec, a complex of buildings founded by Monseigneur François de Laval in 1663. The adjacent Basilique-Cathédrale Notre-Dame-de-Québec, Chapelle des Jésuites and other magnificent churches and cathedrals are treasure troves of exquisite religious art.

City Insider

Words to the wise
The Quebec City Museum Card provides free or discounted admission to two dozen museums and attractions over three days, including free public bus transportation within city limits.

Locals love it
A 32-kilometre walking trail along the St. Charles River connects several historical sites and parks that offer year-round recreation and great birdwatching.

How long to stay
A four day trip allows ample time to sightsee and to sample the restaurants and recreational pursuits.

What's nearby
Côte-de-Beaupré.

When to go
Most of the major festivals take place in summer, although Winter Carnival, held between late January and mid-February, is an experience not to be missed.

Time to Relax
North America's oldest shopping district, Quartier Petit-Champlain is a mix of boutiques and bistros on pedestrianized streets. It's one of the city's best areas to shop for native crafts including sculptures, weavings and jewellery. Quebecers like to eat and the city does not disappoint. Diners can find everything from innovative cuisine to internationally inspired choices to Québéçois fare including caribou. Among its many parks is the Plains of Abraham, the site of a pivotal battle in 1759 that shaped North America's future. It's a favourite with cyclists in summer and cross-country skiers in winter. The city also has an aquarium that displays marine creatures from around the world.

Around Quebec City

ÎLE D'ORLÉANS

Discovered by Jacques Cartier in 1535, the 34-kilometre island, attached to the mainland by bridge, was one of the first colonies in New France. Today, inhabitants of its six parishes still farm and fish as their ancestors did. The Saint-Pierre area has the largest concentration of agricultural enterprises, including farms, fruit orchards, vineyards, cider houses and sugar shacks, where patrons can sample maple products. Artisanal cheese is made at Les Fromages de l'isle d'Orléans in Sainte-Famille from 17th-century recipes. The entire island is a designated historic district with more than 600 heritage buildings, including its oldest church Église St-Pierre, built in 1717. Tours of Manoir Mauvide-Genest provide insight into life during the French regime. At La Forge à Pique-Assaut visitors can learn about an early iron foundry, while Parc maritime de Saint-Laurent-de-l'Île d'Orléans, a former boatyard, chronicles the local maritime heritage. The island also has a place to go dogsledding. More than 80 artisans display their work at local art galleries and studios.

PLANNING

Visit in summer and early autumn when berries and fruit are available at local farms and farm stands.

MONTMORENCY FALLS

Since first noted on geographical maps in 1613 by French explorer Samuel de Champlain, people have been flocking to Montmorency Falls, just minutes from Old Quebec, to stand in awe of their raging power and spectacular setting. At 83 metres high, the falls are 30 metres higher than Niagara Falls. Parc de la Chute-Montmorency offers several options for viewing the falls as they plunge over a rocky cliff into the St. Lawrence River. A cable car travels to the top to Manoir Montmorency, a recreation of the summer villa built on this site in 1780 for Sir Frederick Haldimand, then governor of Quebec. The building houses an interpretive centre and restaurant where diners can enjoy amazing views of the falls and deep river gorge. On summer nights the cascades are illuminated. Winter provides a stunningly different vista, when the water freezes, creating a toboggan run and cliff for ice climbers.

PLANNING

Go in midsummer when the park hosts the annual Loto-Québec International Fireworks Competition, a three-week long spectacle.

Unhurried pace Although only minutes from Quebec City's modern downtown, Île d'Orléans' centuries-old buildings put it in a different time and place.

Getting up close Visitors can cross the suspension footbridge over Montmorency Falls or descend a staircase with observation platforms along the cliff.

SAINTE-ANNE-DE-BEAUPRÉ

One of Canada's most beloved sacred sites, Basilique Sainte-Anne-de-Beaupré dominates the townscape in Sainte-Anne-de-Beaupré, 20 kilometres east of Quebec City. It honours Saint Anne, the patron saint of shipwrecked sailors, and is built where sailors caught in a storm in 1650 safely made it to shore. Construction of the present neo-Romanesque edifice, built from granite, began in 1928. It is the fifth and most elaborate church to be built on the site. The basilica includes 22 chapels and 18 altars, many dedicated to important Catholic saints. Every inch of its magnificent dome-vaulted ceiling is covered with mosaics portraying scenes of Saint Anne's life. Intricately carved wooden pews, magnificent murals and exquisite statues embellish the basilica's interior. Exhibits at a small museum nearby recount the history of both the saint and the shrine from the original chapel built in 1658 to the modern-day basilica. The collection includes several 17th- and 18th-century religious paintings and gifts left by pilgrims. The grounds also include a commemorative chapel, built in 1878, and Scala Santa, a replica of the Holy Stairs in Rome that pilgrims climb on bended knees.

PLANNING

The peak pilgrimage period is around July 26, the feast of Sainte Anne. The basilica may be visited year-round, but the museum and other religious sites are open just in summer.
🏛 ⛪ 🖼

RÉSERVE FAUNIQUE DU CAP TOURMENTE

The arrival of autumn on the northern shore of the St. Lawrence River brings snow geese in flocks numbering in the thousands. More than 800,000 geese stop in the bulrush marshes along Réserve faunique du Cap Tourmente on their 4,000-kilometre migration from their summer nesting grounds in the Canadian Arctic. The reserve, a major ornithological site in Canada, is near Saint-Joachim, about 50 kilometres east of Quebec City. Le Bois-sent-bon Trail, a 1.3-kilometre loop from the interpretive centre, leads to the marshes where the snow geese feed. Other trails in the 18-kilometre network have habitats favoured by more than 300 bird species, including warblers and other migratory species. Peregrine falcons may be spotted on the cliffs, while mallards, northern shovelers and other wading ducks may be found in ponds, especially in spring. The reserve is open in winter for birdwatching and other activities. Feeding stations along some trails attract woodpeckers, jays and other winter residents.

PLANNING

The best time to observe snow geese is in early October, during peak migration time.
🌲 👫 ⛺ 🐦

Luminous views The last of the 240 stained-glassed windows were installed in the present Basilique Sainte-Anne-de-Beaupré in the 1940s.

QUEBEC WINTER CARNIVAL

The annual Carnaval de Quebec embraces the winter season with a whirlwind of festivities and a massive ice palace constructed in the heart of Quebec City for Bonhomme, the carnival's snowman-king and mascot. Night parades, snow sculptures, giant snow slides and sleigh, dogsled and ice-canoe races enthrall visitors at the world's largest winter carnival. Musical performances and hearty Québéçois fare, including the potent alcoholic drink Caribou, round out the 17-day pre-Lenten celebration.

Planning:
Most major events are scheduled during the three weekends of Carnival in late January and February. Book hotel reservations early and bring warm clothes as most activities take place outdoors.

Between Quebec and Montreal

CHEMIN DU ROY

Canada's first highway, known as the King's Road, meanders past farm fields and delightful villages, many of which are part of the Most Beautiful Villages of Quebec network. Built in 1737 to link New France's three largest cities—Montreal, Trois-Rivières and Quebec City—it provides a slower-paced alternative for travel in the region. The road mainly follows Route 138, which parallels the St. Lawrence River, for 280 kilometres from Repentigny near Montreal to Saint-Augustin-de-Desmaures just outside Quebec City. Several sections of the road are part of La Route Verte, a 4,000-kilometre provincial bikeway popular with cyclists.

PLANNING

The route is well signposted with the symbol of a crown, and there are plenty of historical sites and museums to visit along the way.

MAURICIE

Parc national de la Mauricie's forested grandeur is equalled only by its other natural attractions, including its vast plateaux, plunging waterfalls, lush river valleys and more than 150 pristine lakes and rivers. Located halfway between Montreal and Quebec City, the 536-square-kilometre park has no shortage of activities for outdoor enthusiasts. It offers backcountry access on

Laurentian Mountain trails for the hard-core hiker and an expansive network of paths for day hikers and mountain bikers. Close to 180 bird species, including 12 species of raptors, have been observed in the park while sightings of moose by canoeists and canoe-campers along Lac Wapizagonke and other waterways are not uncommon. Private lodges are available for overnight accommodations on the western shore of Lac à la Pêche. The park can also be enjoyed by car on a 63-kilometre drive from Saint-Mathieu to Saint-Jean-des-Piles.

PLANNING

Summer is the most popular time to visit, but with more than 90 percent of the park covered with forests, autumn brings splendid autumnal colours.

TROIS-RIVIÈRES

From its beginnings in 1634 as a fur-trading post, Trois-Rivières became Canada's first industrial city when it established an iron foundry 100 years later. Today, it enjoys a reputation as a cultural city with cafés, art galleries and museums. Le Musée québécois de culture populaire on the edge of the historic quarter features exhibits on Québécois folk art and popular culture. The adjacent Old Prison of Trois-Rivières, built in 1822, offers tours and overnight stays. The history lessons continue at the Forges du Saint-Maurice National Historic Site of Canada, the early ironworks, and at

Autumnal treat Colourful foliage frames the view of Lac Wapizagonke from an observation deck in Parc national de la Mauricie.

Monastère des Ursulines by the waterfront. The original monastery building, one of the city's oldest structures, dates to 1699. Its 1715 chapel is open to the public, as is a museum with items used by the nuns.

PLANNING
The city hosts a music festival in summer and poetry and dance festivals in autumn.
🏃 🏛 🖼

DESCHAMBAULT-GRONDINES
Signs of the past are present everywhere in Deschambault-Grondines. This is where Jacques Cartier stopped on his second North American voyage and where Samuel de Champlain chose to build a fur-trading post in 1633. The municipality, a merger of two historic villages in 2002, has a rich religious heritage that can be explored through sites such as an early 19th-century presbytery and

Bygone days The largest concentration of charming old buildings in Trois-Rivières, which survived a huge fire in 1908, are near the waterfront.

two mid-19th-century churches designed by architect Thomas Baillairgé—Église Saint-Joseph de Deschambault and Église Saint-Charles-Borromée. Centre d'interprétation du Chemin du Roy includes an interesting exhibit on the highway's history. Two of the oldest windmills in North America, Chemin Sir-Lomer-Gouin and Moulin à vent de Grondines, also are found here. The latter, built in 1674, houses an exhibit of the windmill's past, first as a flour mill and later as a lighthouse to help ships navigate the treacherous river rapids. Moulin de La Chevrotière, a mill situated at Deschambault's western end, dates to 1802. It contains numerous historical exhibits as well as a gallery featuring contemporary art. The mill's nature trails along the river are ideal for discovering local plants and birds.

PLANNING
Although the museums are open only in summer, the area's historic architecture can be viewed year-round.
🌲 🏛 🖼 🐦

Step back into the 19th century Vieux Presbytère, built in 1815 on Cap Lauzon, is typical of the buildings found in Deschambault-Grondines.

CAP-SANTÉ
First settled in the late 17th century, Cap-Santé has an exceptional number of well-preserved 18th-century buildings. Many can be found along Vieux Chemin, which was once part of Chemin du Roy and is now considered one of Canada's prettiest streets. Cap-Santé saw action during the Seven Years' War when Fort Jacques-Cartier was built nearby at the mouth of the Jacques-Cartier River to hold back the British on their march to Montreal. The war disrupted the construction of Église Sainte-Famille, one of the last churches built under the French regime. Construction began in 1754 but was halted when its building materials were requisitioned by the fort. The twin-towered church with its impressive baroque interior was completed in 1767. Surrounded by fields and picturesque views of the St. Lawrence River, today Cap-Santé is a quiet farming village. Its architecture is its main attraction, but it also has an interpretation centre that describes the salmon migration on the river.

PLANNING
Visit in June for Riche en couleurs, an art festival, or in late November for Noël d'Antan, an old-fashioned Christmas celebration.
🏛 🖼 🖼

A Dozen Great Hikes in Quebec

Canyon Sainte-Anne

An unforgettable hiking experience awaits visitors in this private family-friendly park. With its impressive 74-metre waterfall, swirling waters and spectacular geological formations, Canyon Sainte-Anne in Saint-Joachim, 40 kilometres from Quebec City, is one of eastern Quebec's recreational jewels.

A one-mile walking trail traverses the deep chasm, carved from 1.2-billion-year-old rock by erosion during two ice ages and the rushing waters of the Sainte-Anne River. Visitors can expect to climb a lot of stairs, although a special shuttle tour is available for the disabled.

Starting at the head of the falls where the roaring river begins its plunge into the rocky gorge, the trail hugs the steep, tree-lined canyon walls as it winds its way slowly down to the canyon floor. Three suspension bridges—one of which is the highest in Quebec—and several observation decks offer a progression of different views of the falls and its natural features, including the 21-metre Giant's Kettle pothole and smaller cascades, as well as rainbows in the mist on sunny days.

At midpoint, hikers have the option of crossing over the McNicoll Bridge, named for brothers Jean-Marie and Laurent McNicoll, who

developed the trail in the early 1970s. Located 60 metres above the water, the crossing offers dramatic views of the canyon and falls as does Rocky Flats, a popular picnic spot. The canyon may also be explored by zip lining, rappelling and rock climbing.

Planning: Go in October when the autumnal colours are at their most glorious, or in spring for the wildflowers. Adventure activities are available from May through October. Picnic areas are located near the main building and by the river.

Other Great Hikes

La Pinède Trail, Parc national du Bic, Bas-Saint-Laurent. Said to have some of the world's finest sunsets, the trail and lookouts offer amazing views of Anse à l'Orignal and Anse à Mouille-Cul, two beautiful coves on the St. Lawrence River.

Cap-Tourmente Trail, Sentier des Caps de Charlevoix, Charlevoix. A favourite of birdwatchers for its thousands of migrating snow geese in autumn and spring, this route to the top of Cap Tourmente does not disappoint when it comes to scenic vistas.

Les Graves Trail, Forillon National Park, Gaspé. Following the Gaspé Bay to the tip of Cap-Gaspé, the trail passes through Grande-Grave National Historic Site, which has two historic cemeteries and a well-preserved homestead, where generations of fishermen-farmers once lived.

Mont Saint-Alban Trail, Forillon National Park, Gaspé. A three-hour hike to the summit of 283-metre Mont Saint-Alban promises 360-degree views of the Gulf of St. Lawrence with the province of New Brunswick and the Anticosti Islands in the distance.

Lac aux Américains Trail, Parc national de la Gaspésie, Gaspé. Ideal for novice hikers, this five-hour walk in boreal forest to a glacial lake offers plenty of opportunities for bird- and wildlife watching.

Mont-Ernest-Laforce Trail, Parc national de la Gaspésie, Gaspé. This easy loop with great views of Mont-Albert and Mont Olivine is best accessed at sunrise, when moose commonly forage in the area.

Le Perdreau Trail, Jacques-Cartier National Park. As popular with snowshoers as it is with day hikers, this 5-kilometre loop traverses dense maple forests and a glacial valley, finding its way to Lac Buvard, the perfect place to stop for a rest.

Le Lac-Poisson Trail, Parc national du Mont-Tremblant, Laurentians. Winding through deciduous forests and past cliffs in the Laurentian wilderness, this trail's long, steep grade challenges, then rewards hikers with a dip in a solitary, pristine lake and walk to a nearby waterfall.

Lusk Cave Trail, Gatineau Park, Laurentians. A favourite hike for families, it offers a chance to explore a 12,500-year-old marble cave by flashlight, with a return trip that hugs the Lac Philippe shoreline.

De La Rivière Matane Trail, Réserve Faunique de Matane, Matane. This easy walk follows the river, past waterfalls, into the centre of a wildlife refuge known for its large moose population as well as deer, black bears and coyotes.

The Statue Trail, Saguenay National Park. The steep trail heads to the Cap Trinité summit with spectacular views of the Saguenay Fjord en route and a 9-metre-high Our Lady of the Saguenay statue, erected in 1881, at the top.

Touring the Eastern Townships

SHERBROOKE

With an economy based on the food, textile and mechanical industries, Sherbrooke grew from a small 19th-century mill town to the sixth largest city in Quebec. It's a vibrant place with a host of art galleries, festivals, recreational sports and museums, including the Musée des beaux-arts de Sherbrooke and the Musée de la nature et des sciences se Sherbrooke. The city's history is told through guided walking tours of the Quartier du Vieux-Nord and a series of fresco murals on public buildings. Cyclists can explore Sherbrooke on the 126-kilometre Grandes-Fourches cycling network that travels along the Magog and Saint-François rivers. Lac Magog and Lac des Nations provide numerous options for water sports. With winter's arrival, attention turns to cross-country and alpine skiing at Parc du Mont-Bellevue as well as ice skating at Lac des Nations. A nearby restored train depot houses a marketplace with an outdoor farmers' market in summer. The Ordford Express departs near here on scenic excursions to Magog and Eastman.

PLANNING
Sherbrooke is a year-round destination with museums and attractions open throughout the year and different sports and activities for every season.
👭 🏛 🖼 🛷 ⛵ 🦌 🐦

Historic charm The Holy Trinity Anglican Church, built in 1880, is one of the 19th-century Catholic and Anglican churches that still stand in Frelighsburg.

FRELIGHSBURG

Tucked against the foot of Pinnacle Mountain in a bucolic river valley, the beautiful village of Frelighsburg is as well known for its locally produced fruits and specialty food products as it is for its architectural gems. Many of its 19th-century buildings still stand, including its town hall and an 1839 mill, erected on the Pike River by a son of Abram Freligh, one of the Loyalist founders of the town. The historic grammar school has been repurposed as the Arts Centre, displaying works of regional artists, whose paintings and other art can be purchased at town art galleries. Frelighsburg shines when it comes to local foods. It's a prime apple-growing area with farms that sell apples, cider, pies and other products. Honey, vinegar and various meats, including lamb, rabbit and duck, are available at area shops; the wineries, producing both apple and grape wines, including a sweet ice wine, are undeniably one of the area's biggest draws.

PLANNING
Celebrate the arts in early September with Festiv'Art, which is also an ideal time to visit farms for apples.
🏛 🛤 🖼

KNOWLTON

In the heart of Quebec's Eastern Townships, Knowlton exudes charm, with shady tree-lined streets, turreted Victorian homes, art galleries, eateries and museums. Many of its restaurants serve the world-famous Brome Lake duck, a delicacy from a local farm that's been in the duck-raising business since 1912. Gastronomes will also find the town's other local offerings—wines, meats, fruits and lavender-infused foods—reason enough to visit this delightful community on the shores of Lac Brome. Its architecture reflects its

Granby Zoo

When the mayor of Granby, animal lover Pierre-Horace Boivin, established a small zoo in his city in 1953, he never could have imagined that it would grow into an internationally respected zoological park. It's heralded both for its conservation efforts in protecting endangered species and for its informative programs designed to educate the 600,000 annual visitors about its more than 180 different species of animals. Ranked as one of Quebec's top attractions, the zoo, located 84 kilometres from Montreal, also includes an amusement park and the popular Amazoo Waterpark.

anglophone pedigree and Loyalist roots. The largest concentration of historic buildings, including former general stores, a bank and a gristmill workers' tenement house, can be found along Lakeside Road. The Brome County Historical Society Museum also sits on this street. It is comprised of six vintage buildings, including a 1904 fire hall and 1854 school academy that house a collection of artifacts and a First World War Fokker D-VII biplane, one of only three in the world.

PLANNING
Canard en Fête, the famous Brome Lake Duck Festival, takes place in September. In winter the Festival of Lights illuminates the town.
🏛 ⛷ 🖼 ⛵

STANBRIDGE-EAST
The well-maintained clapboard and brick homes that line Stanbridge-East's streets appear unchanged from a century ago. Add to that tranquil Brochets River, a favourite with paddlers, and it is understandable why the village is considered one of the prettiest in the Eastern Townships. The Missisquoi Museum, which has thousands of artifacts spread over three historic

buildings, recounts the area's past including its Loyalist origins and a mid-19th-century economic boom brought on by the arrival of the railway in the region, resulting in an increase in tanneries, mills and other businesses. Visitors can explore the Cornell Mill, Walbridge Barn and Hodge's General Store, which contains merchandise from the turn of the last century. Stanbridge-East is on the Wine Route, which links more than a dozen wineries in the Townships, including several clustered between the village and Dunham to the east.

PLANNING
Although the wineries are open year-round, Missisquoi Museum closes its doors from mid-October through late May.
👫 🏛 ⛷ ⛵

NORTH HATLEY
With the extension of the railway line in 1880, tourism boomed in North Hatley, turning the quiet town into a bustling summer resort. A slew of hotels and businesses quickly sprung up, catering to the wealthy Americans who made this their summer playground. This cozy village about 32 kilometres north of the U.S. border continues to attract vacationers who want to browse the art galleries and boutiques or canoe, fish or enjoy a guided boat tour of the 16-kilometre-long pristine glacial lake. In summer and autumn The Piggery presents plays, concerts and other theatrical performances in a converted pig barn. Visitors can also savour foods from local farms, including creamy Québécois cheeses, duck foie gras, smoked lake trout and apple cider. The Abbaye Saint-Benoît-du-Lac on nearby Lake Memphremagog is famous for its L'Ermite blue cheese, which

Water views North Hatley is situated on the northern tip of Lake Massawippi, making it an ideal location for vacationers.

Cornell Mill The bulk of the Missisquoi Museum's 12,000 artifacts can be viewed in this three-storey brick gristmill, built in Stanbridge East in 1830.

also appears on restaurant menus along with other products produced by the resident Benedictine monks.

PLANNING
Try a quiet winter getaway for horseback riding or a sleigh ride on snow-packed trails.
⛷ 🖼 ⛵ 🐎

MAPLE SYRUP

As winter loosens its grip and the days get warmer, sap begins to drip from sugar maple trees. In a ritual of spring as old as the early native settlements, sugar makers gather sap by bucket or pipeline, then slowly boil it down into golden syrup in sugar shacks across Quebec. It takes 40 litres of sap to make just one litre of maple syrup, a process that marries long-standing tradition with new technology.

Planning:
Visit a commercial cabane à sucre,
or sugar shack, any time from early
March to mid-April for the complete
maple experience that includes
everything from learning how
syrup is made to sampling
old-style Québéçois cooking
in an all-you-can-eat meal.

Montreal Sights and Sounds

A meld of old-world grandeur and cosmopolitan flair, this island metropolis seduces with its gastronomic offerings, active arts scene and top-drawer attractions.

Bilingual Montreal is hip, yet traditional. While shaped by its past, it's quick to embrace the present and look towards the future. It is a city of contrasts. Modern architecture shares streets with buildings erected three centuries ago. Montreal's

incomparable nightlife revolves around music clubs, restaurants and performing arts venues, notably Place des Arts. The city flaunts its cultural assets with a panoply of remarkable museums, while its green side is evident in the countless parks, gardens and recreational paths throughout the city.

Haute cuisine restaurants mix with delicatessens and inexpensive bistros to offer a vast choice of palate-pleasing fare. The pedestrianized Rue Prince-Arthur and Rue Duluth are full of ethnic restaurants and outdoor cafés combining great cuisine with lively atmosphere for a not-to-be-missed dining treat. For a fun French-Canadian experience, Le Plateau-Mont-Royal and Saint-Denis offer an eclectic choice of local boutiques and French bistros.

Vieux-Montreal

The crooked cobblestone streets and pleasing façades of a battery of heritage greystone buildings entice visitors to explore Vieux-Montreal. This was where the city was born in 1642, when Ville-Marie, a Catholic mission, was founded. The area's oldest surviving building, Saint-Sulpice Seminary,

Towering cityscape Cyclists travelling along the Lachine Canal, a popular bike route in Montreal, will have the chance to enjoy views of the city's modern skyline.

built in 1685, squats next to the highly ornate Gothic revival La Basilique Notre-Dame-de-Montréal, one of North America's largest churches. At the other end of the compact district, Marché Bonsecours, a former government building turned trendy marketplace, competes with Rue Saint-Paul, a narrow cobblestone street bursting with art galleries, boutiques and intimate restaurants. At Place Jacques-Cartier, the historic quarter's central square, street performers entertain for tips as diners applaud from outdoor cafés and calèches—

Food-lover's paradise Busy *boulangeries*, or bakeries, serve a tantalizing range of fresh pastries bound to please even the most finicky of taste buds.

Don't Miss

Pointe-à-Callière
The museum in Vieux-Montreal, near the old port area, helps visitors discover the city's first marketplace, Catholic cemetery and other centuries-old historical remnants through an underground archaeological tour of the actual site of Montreal's birthplace.

The Metro Museum of Art
Elaborate murals, stained-glass windows and other artwork, all part of an enormous planned metro art gallery, await discovery at Montreal's many metro stations.

Jean-Talon Market
At North America's largest open-air market, stalls overflow with fresh produce, smoked meats, fish and cheeses. Visitors are encouraged to stop and taste the wares.

City Insider

Words to the wise
La Vitrine culturelle, a centralized ticket office located on Sainte-Catherine Street, offers tickets for upcoming shows and events including last-minute, half-priced tickets.

Locals love it
The city's 500-kilometre network of bike paths provides access to the riverfront, shopping districts, museums and other attractions.

How long to stay
Many of the city's major attractions can be visited in three or four days, but a longer stay provides more time to explore.

What's nearby
The Laurentians; Parc national d'Oka.

When to go
Winter brings unexpected pleasures with its recreational pursuits and festivals but summer offers the best opportunities to experience all that the city has to offer.

horse-drawn carriages—wait for their next fare. Vieux-Port, just down the hill, provides riverfront access for recreation, boat cruises and the innovative Montreal Science Centre.

Arts and Culture
Montreal is often referred to as "Canada's Cultural Capital," and for good reason. Its innumerable museums showcase famous artworks, scientific and technological discoveries, cultural treasures and historic artifacts from Canada and around the world. Musée des beaux-arts de Montréal is recognized as the country's first art museum and one of its finest. Its galleries present works by European Impressionists, Inuit and First Nations artists, Canadian landscape painters and others as well as displays of decorative arts. Musée d'art contemporain de Montréal features paintings, sculptures and other works by contemporary artists. The museum is part of the Place des Arts complex with its resident opera and ballet companies and symphony orchestra. The Canadian Centre for Architecture, housed in an elegant 19th-century home with a modern stone addition, is a ten-minute walk away. The city also counts a number of historical sites among its cultural offerings.

A View from the Top
A sea of gleaming skyscrapers, high-rise apartment buildings and massive cathedrals punctuates Montreal's skyline, a view best

Lachine Canal National Historic Site features a 14-kilometre bicycle trail and guided canal boat tours. Montreal also has a number of fine zoos including the Ecomuseum Zoo with species native to Quebec's St. Lawrence Valley and the Biôdome near the botanic gardens.

Island Playgrounds

Bustling Montreal has its own island playground in the middle of the St. Lawrence River known as Parc Jean-Drapeau, which encompasses Expo 67's two islands. On

enjoyed from above. The city's highest point, 234-metre-high Mont Royal in Parc du Mont-Royal, also offers the best panoramic views. The park was designed by Frederick Law Olmsted, the same architect responsible for New York City's Central Park, and is a haven for walkers, picnickers, birdwatchers and cross-country skiers. The mountain is also home to Oratoire Saint-Joseph's, a destination for pilgrims from around the world. At its foot lies the Golden Square Mile, a stretch of the city's wealthiest

Autumn festivities The La Magie des Lanternes festival in the Chinese Gardens at the botanical gardens is renowned for its colourful display.

mansions. The views also are superb from the Montreal Tower in the Olympic Stadium. The tower lookout of the 300-year-old Chapelle Notre-Dame-de-Bonsecours in Vieux-Montreal, a pilgrimage site for sailors, offers vistas worth the climb as does the Sailors' Memorial Clock Tower that overlooks the St. Lawrence River, the city and the Vieux-Port quays.

Green Spaces

Urban Montreal has a pastoral side with more than 30 parks offering recreation and relaxation. Its jewel is the Jardin botanique de Montréal, which has tens of thousands of plant species in 30 themed outdoor gardens and ten exhibition greenhouses. Its Insectarium features North American insects and butterflies. At the city's eastern end, Parc-nature de la Pointe-aux-Prairies includes 261 hectares of marshland and maple forests supporting nearly 200 bird species. Birdwatching is also popular at Parc-nature de l'Île-de-la-Visitation, along with hiking, bicycling, snowshoeing and tobogganing. The Sault-au-Récollet Historic Site in the park treats visitors to a look at a 280-year-old historic mill village. The

Taking in the view For outstanding vistas of Montreal's skyline, stop along the Kondiaronk Belvedere in Parc du Mont-Royal.

Île Sainte-Hélène visitors can wander past buildings from the famous world's fair with a stop at the Biosphere. Built as the American Pavilion, the geodesic dome now houses an interactive museum of hydrology with a focus on environmental issues and responsible consumption. Musée Stewart, a former British garrison, contains maps, vintage weaponry and other artifacts from the earliest military encampments to the mid-19th century. A highlight in summer is the daily military parade. La Ronde Amusement Park nearby features the world's highest wooden roller coaster and summer concerts and fireworks. On Île Notre-Dame the French and Quebec pavilions from Expo 67 saw new life as the Casino de Montréal. The island also sees action in summer when top international racers compete at Circuit Gilles-Villeneuve, a demanding Formula One Grand Prix racetrack.

Ville de Festivals

In Montreal festivals are almost a way of life. La Fete des Nieges, the biggest winter festival, kicks off the year with a host of fun outdoor activities from skating, zip lining and tubing to snow and ice sculpture contests in a carnival-like atmosphere in Parc Jean-Drapeau. The park's Snow Village, a complex of buildings crafted from ice and snow, including a hotel, igloos, a restaurant and lighted snow tunnels, stays open all winter long.

In summer the calendar swells with festivals and events. Les FrancoFolies de Montréal, the largest music festival in the French-speaking world, is followed by Just For Laughs, a showcase of comedic talent, and the spectacular International Festival of Circus Arts. (Montreal does have ties with the internationally acclaimed Cirque du Soleil.) Jazz lovers are treated to Festival International de Jazz de Montréal, one the many musical events that occur throughout the year. Autumn brings the internationally acclaimed La Magie des Lanternes, a two-month long spectacle that illuminates the Chinese Garden at the botanical gardens with thousands of paper lanterns.

Underground City

Montrealers don't worry about inclement weather interfering with their work or play. La Ville Souterraine, or the underground city, gives them sheltered access to more than 1,700 stores and several hotels, restaurants, movie theatres and cultural venues. The 30 kilometres of boutique-lined corridors connect to metro stations and other public transportation as well as apartment complexes and office buildings. The subterranean city was conceived in 1962 when an underground passage was built during the construction of Place Ville-Marie, the city's first skyscraper.

Olympic record Built in 1976 for the Olympic Games, the Montreal Olympic Stadium supports the highest inclined tower in the world, standing at 175 metres.

Day Trips from Montreal

OKA MONASTERY

When the army of the French Third Republic seized the Abbey of Bellefontaine in France in 1880, eight Trappist monks fled to start a new Cistercian chapter in Canada. Offered land in Oka, 55 kilometres northwest of Montreal, they harvested wood from the forests on Saint Sulpice hill to build their first monastery and turned to agriculture, including cheese making, to support the order. The Abbey of Notre-Dame du Lac, known as the Oka Abbey, grew to include a main greystone monastery building with gardens, a neo-Romanesque abbey church and several outbuildings on 270 hectares. Although the order moved in 2009, the abbey shop still sells jellies, cider, honey, chocolate and the order's famous Oka cheese. Made from a recipe that the first monks brought from France, this cow's milk cheese has a pungent aroma and soft creamy flavour. The Calvaire d'Oka Trail in nearby Parc national d'Oka takes in the Calvaire with its stone chapels and extraordinary views of the Lake of Two Mountains and New York's Adirondacks.

PLANNING

The Oka Ferry provides frequent ferry service across the Lake of Two Mountains between Hudson and Oka.

🌲 🛶

MONT-TREMBLANT

The pretty mountain village of Mont-Tremblant on the shores of Lac Mercier is a gateway to a four-season recreational paradise. While its amenities, including restaurants, antique shops, boutiques and a train-depot art gallery, give it an identity of its own, it also provides access to Mont-Tremblant Resort, a renowned ski resort that includes the Laurentians' two highest peaks, and Le P'tit Train du Nord Linear Park. The latter, a 232-kilometre recreational path for walkers, bikers, skaters and winter-sports enthusiasts, follows an abandoned rail bed from Bois-des-Filion north to Mont-Laurier. The area's pièce de résistance is the 1,510-square-kilometre Parc national du Mont-Tremblant, Quebec's first national park. Its multiple lakes, including Lac Monroe, which is popular for recreational activities, and the Diable River are ideal for kayaking and canoeing, while backpackers and hikers will find an extensive network of trails that do double duty in winter for snowshoe and cross-country ski treks. While not always easy to spot, wolverines, moose, black bears and wolves make their home here, as do the more frequently observed otters and foxes. Many lakes host colonies of beavers and their well-engineered lodges.

PLANNING

Although this is ski country, summer and autumn offer a wide array of choices for outdoor activities including golfing.

🌲 🛶 🦅 🎿 🛷

A run with a view Mont-Tremblant, the highest peak in the Laurentians, receives an average total snowfall of 380 centimetres per year.

Illuminated splendour Église Saint-Sauveur-des-Monts, a church with twin spires and a spectacular steeple, was built between 1903 and 1904.

SAINT-SAUVEUR-DES-MONTS

The village of Saint-Sauveur-des-Monts is considered the birthplace of the Quebec ski industry. Although skiers from Montreal, just 60 kilometres to the south, had been making their way to the Laurentians since the early 1900s, their numbers increased greatly in the 1920s when the snow train, Le P'tit Train du Nord, began carrying Montrealers to the winter ski slopes. What cemented Saint-Sauveur's claim was the installation of the first permanent ski lift in 1934, followed 14 years later by the first T-bar in North America. The history of skiing in the region is chronicled through exhibits and a skiers' Hall of Fame at the Laurentian Ski Museum in the former Saint-Sauveur fire station, opposite the lovely Église Saint-Sauveur-des-Monts, the Catholic church in the village centre. Although Mont Saint-Sauveur, blessed with one of the longest ski seasons in the province, is the area's biggest draw, in summer an outdoor water park, one of Canada's largest, and the annual Festival des Arts de Saint-Sauveur attract large crowds.

PLANNING

Winter is not-to-be-missed ski season, but summer offers a chance to enjoy a slower pace; autumn brings the Fall Colour Festival.
🧑‍🤝‍🧑 🏛 🏞 🎿

SUCRERIE DE LA MONTAGNE

Clouds of steam and the sweet, sticky aroma of maple fill the air as sap is turned into delicate, golden syrup at Sucrerie de la Montagne. Designated an official Quebec Heritage site, the sugar shack is located in the middle of a 50-hectare sugar bush atop Mont Rigaud. Maple sugaring is done the old-fashioned way, using horses and buckets to collect sap and a wood-fired evaporator to boil it down. The buckets are a common sight on the trees surrounding the complex, which includes a bakery, general store, overnight cabins and a 500-seat dining hall. Horse-drawn wagons or sleighs, depending on the season, are available for transporting guests. Served family style, the all-you-can-eat feast offered in the dining hall starts with a bowl of hearty pea soup with ham followed by a parade of platters of maple-smoked ham, baked beans, meatball stew, tourtière, country-style sausages,

Montreal Train Escapades

It's all aboard for Montreal Train Escapades. These themed train adventures feature full-day tours to visit a vineyard or sugar shack, explore a historical site or go apple picking. One trip for true rail buffs goes to Exporail, Canada's largest railway museum, in Saint-Constant, south of the city. Operated by the Agence métropolitaine de transport, which oversees the city's commuter trains, excursions are offered from March through October and leave from Gare Centrale in Montreal.

mashed potatoes, crusty breads and other Québécois foods, most cooked with maple. Traditional sugar pie and pancakes with maple syrup cap off the meal.

PLANNING

Although open year-round, the sugaring season from late winter to early spring provides an opportunity to observe the whole process from collecting sap by bucket with horses to boiling it into syrup.
🧑‍🤝‍🧑 🏛

Dining in style Fiddlers and musicians get toes tapping for a night of dancing and singing, adding to the ambiance at Sucrerie de la Montagne.

A Dozen Great Churches in Quebec

La Basilique Notre-Dame-de-Montréal

The basilica's lavish interior featuring intricate stained-glass windows, art masterpieces and a towering hand-carved wooden altarpiece attracts hundreds of thousands of visitors from around the world each year. The impressive Gothic revival church is an architectural marvel, with 69-metre-high twin towers that rise dramatically over Le Place d'Armes in Vieux-Montreal. The building was designed by American architect James O'Donnell, an Irish Protestant who later converted to Catholicism so he could have his funeral in the church. Most of the construction was completed between 1824 and 1829.

The interior has elaborate, decorative woodwork motifs carved by hand from rare woods. Victor Bourgeau, a Montreal architect, designed the high altar, choir stalls and altarpiece during a renovation in the 1870s. The statues were sculpted by French artist Henri Bouriché and the pulpit by the renowned artist Louis-Philippe Hébert. The vaulted-dome ceilings are painted a sea of blue dotted with thousands of gold stars. The stained-glass windows, imported from Limoges, France, represent scenes not from the bible, but from Montreal's religious history. The basilica is home to a 7,000-pipe Casavant Frères organ, with pipes ranging from 10 metres to only 6 millimetres.

Behind the main altar lies the smaller Chapelle du Sacré-Coeur, so in demand for weddings that couples wait up to two years to wed there. The main sanctuary often hosts funerals of prominent people, although the only person ever buried in the crypt was O'Donnell, who did not live to see the work finished.

Planning: Although regular guided tours are offered at the basilica, scheduled activities are suspended at times for religious ceremonies such as weddings, funerals and special events.

Other Great Churches

Église Sainte-Famille de Cap-Santé, Cap-Santé. Declared a historical monument in 1986, this church has a lovely façade. Its baroque interior is a well-preserved example of French regime architecture.

Basilique Cathédrale Marie-Reine-du-Monde, Montreal. This impressive Roman Catholic cathedral, finished in 1894, is a one-third-size replica of Rome's St. Peter's Basilica, with a gated crypt containing the tombs of many of Montreal's cardinals and archbishops.

Chapelle Notre Dame-de-Bonsecours, Montreal. One of Montreal's oldest churches, it is called the Sailors Church because seafarers arriving at Vieux-Port in the 19th century prayed here for a safe voyage.

Église de La Visitation de la Bienheureuse-Vierge-Marie du Sault-au-Récollet, Montreal. Dating back to the French regime, this massive stone church is the oldest on the island of Montreal. It has twin towers and still retains its mid-18th to 19th-century interior décor.

Oratoire Saint-Joseph, Montreal. Founded in 1904, the tiny chapel grew to be the largest shrine in the world dedicated to Saint Joseph. Its dome is the world's second largest, after St. Peter's Basilica in Rome.

Église Saint-François-de-Sales, Neuville. The church is renowned for its religious artworks by François Baillargé and its carved wood baldachin, or canopy, built in 1695, the only one of its kind in Quebec.

Basilique Cathédrale Notre-Dame-de-Québec, Quebec City. North America's oldest parish, this basilica has a stunning interior, including vibrant stained-glass windows and gold-plated altar. It is the burial place of several former bishops and governors.

Église Saint-Roch, Quebec City. At 80 metres long and 46 metres high, it is the largest church in Quebec City. Built in 1881, it sports an impressive Gothic exterior of black granite from nearby Rivière-à-Pierre and a neo-Roman interior of Saskatchewan marble.

Notre-Dame-des-Victoires, Quebec City. A treasure with centuries-old artworks and historic tabernacle, the 300-year-old church was erected at Place-Royale on the site of Samuel de Champlain's "l'Abitation."

Cathédrale de Trois-Rivières, Trois-Rivières. The Cathedral of Trois-Rivières, inaugurated in 1858, contains 125 remarkable stained-glass windows, considered among the finest in Canada, created by Guido Nincheri, an internationally acclaimed liturgical artist from Montreal.

Sanctuaire Notre-Dame-du-Cap, Trois-Rivières. More than 250,000 people make a pilgrimage here annually to admire the original 1714 chapel, one of Canada's oldest, and worship at the modern basilica, with its magnificent stained-glass windows and imposing Casavant organ.

Western Quebec

CANADIAN MUSEUM OF CIVILIZATION

A repository of Canada's human history and cultural diversity, the Gatineau-based museum's exhibits span 20,000 years of habitation, beginning with the Vikings' arrival and continuing to the present day. Designed by prominent Canadian architect Douglas Cardinal, the museum's architectural style captures the essence of Canada's diverse physical landscape. The Grand Hall, lined with Pacific Northwest totem poles and recreated native dwellings, leads into the First Peoples Hall, with exhibits detailing the history of Canada's aboriginal peoples. The Canadian Personalities Hall introduces influential entrepreneurs, explorers, activists, writers and leaders. A series of recreated scenes, some with authentic artifacts, portray everyday life through the centuries in the Canada Hall, among these a circa-1560 Basque whaling station, New France town square, late-19th-century Ontario town's main street and 1970s airport lounge. The building also houses the Canadian Postal Museum, Canadian Children's Museum and an IMAX Theatre, along with temporary exhibits.

PLANNING

Open year-round, the museum makes a great rainy day activity. Check the events calendar for special programs, lectures and exhibits and plan accordingly.
🧍‍♂️ 🏛 🖼

JACQUES CARTIER

Named for the French explorer who stumbled upon this site in his quest for the Northwest Passage, Jacques Cartier Park is an oasis of green in an urban setting with a large number of trails for walkers and hikers. Its strategic location in the heart of Gatineau makes it well-situated to host Canada Day events and the ever-popular Winterlude, a festive three-week celebration of winter that occurs in February. The park hugs the banks of the Ottawa River with views of the downtown and Rideau Falls. The riverfront walkway between Alexandra Bridge and King Edward Bridge provides teasing views of Parliament Hill and the Ottawa skyline. Its connection to Leamy Lake and the Gatineau River makes it ideal for water sports, although the 23-hectare park is a favourite for cyclists as well as snowshoers and cross-country skiers. Hull's oldest surviving house, Maison Charron, built by the city's founder, Philemon Wright, is located in the park.

Suspended staircase The Grand Hall in the Canadian Museum of Civilization is impressive, with huge totem poles and other works of art at every turn.

Summer retreat A walk around the Mackenzie King Estate in Gatineau Park takes visitors past beautiful gardens, picturesque ruins and original cottages.

Winterlude with its Snowflake Kingdom and big snow playground makes the perfect family outing.

🌲 🧑‍🤝‍🧑 🪑 🐦 🛷 🐕‍🦺 🦅

GATINEAU PARK

With more than 50 lakes, vast forests and diverse flora and fauna, Gatineau Park seems more like a wilderness reserve than a park only minutes away from Canada's bustling capital city of Ottawa. Set in the Gatineau Hills, the 361-square-kilometre park is a quick escape for city residents and travellers visiting the region. They can take advantage of its 165 kilometres of trails for warm-weather hiking and 90 kilometres for mountain biking or its many lakes for boating and fishing. Visitors can also explore Lusk Cave, a crystalline limestone cavern. The park remains open in winter, too.

Gatineau Park has more than 50 mammal species, nearly 230 bird species and several plant species found nowhere else in the province. The Mackenzie King Estate near Kingsmere Lake was once the summer home

of William Lyon Mackenzie King, Canada's tenth prime minister. Touring the estate's heritage gardens, trails and buildings is a nice alternative to exploring nature.

PLANNING
Admire the colours at the Fall Rhapsody festival, generally held the first two weeks of October, or go for the solitude in winter on a snowshoe or cross-country ski trek.

🌲 🧑‍🤝‍🧑 🪑 🐦 🛷 🐕‍🦺 🦅

VAL D'OR

The discovery of gold in 1923 put Val d'Or, French for "Valley of Gold," on the map. Although this precious metal is still mined in the area today, it is the community's other outdoor treasures that bring visitors to this western Quebec town. Cité de l'Or ("City of Gold") provides an introduction to the local mining industry through tours of the closed Lamaque Mine, once the richest gold mine in Quebec, including a descent 91 metres below ground to tour the mine shafts. The attraction also offers an interpretive tour of the Village minier de Bourlamaque, a historic mining village that was once the company town for the mine, and a visit to an assay laboratory where ore is turned into liquid gold and then into bars. A popular spot for outdoor sports, Val d'Or is on a snowmobile trail network as well as the 3,600-kilometre-long cross-provincial bike route.

PLANNING
Spectators are welcome for the Tour de l'Abitibi, held in July, where cyclists dash through the tunnels at Cité de l'Or on one leg of a challenging multi-day race.

🌲 🧑‍🤝‍🧑 🏛 🪑 🎿

FORT TÉMISCAMINGUE

Set on Lake Timiskaming's tranquil shores, Fort Témiscamingue-Obedjiwan was situated at a major crossroads on Quebec's main fur-trading route. The original trading

Golden history Visitors to Val d'Or can have an up-close experience with the machinery once used to remove gold from the local mines.

post, built by the French in 1679, was destroyed by the Iroquois less than a decade later and not rebuilt until 1720. It was here that the natives traded beaver pelts for supplies, first with the French and later the British, as the two countries battled to gain possession of the area. At the Fort Témiscamingue-Obedjiwan National Historic Site of Canada, Jean-Baptiste the Voyageur and other 17th- and 18th-century historical characters show visitors how to barter and trade furs, light fires without matches and other crucial skills to survive at the isolated fort. Traditional Algonquin culture is shared through demonstrations of basket weaving and construction of birch-bark canoes and wigwams. A walk along the 1-kilometre Enchanted Forest Trail reveals a grove of eastern white cedars, their strangely twisted trunks created by strong winds.

PLANNING
Visit during one of the summer events such as "Rendez-vous des Voyageurs," which features a period encampment with traditional foods.

🌲 🧑‍🤝‍🧑 🏛 🪑

ONTARIO

Discover Cultural Ottawa

Canada's capital city is home to the prime minister and almost a million people—and also to some of the country's best museums, galleries and festivals.

Although it is the seat of parliament and host to international dignitaries, Ottawa's personality is far from stiff and formal. Instead, the city's atmosphere is fresh and welcoming, as it swings open the doors of its numerous cultural and natural attractions.

Cultural Pursuits

Many of Ottawa's museums and galleries are near the town centre, giving visitors a chance to explore the city's streets and parks. The

National Gallery is one of the best spots to hit on the museum/gallery trail. Designed by Moshe Safdie and situated near the Ottawa River, the gallery is a remarkable piece of art in its own right. Soaring cathedral ceilings and walls of glass greet visitors in the Great Hall. Inside, the permanent collection has works from a vast range of Canadian and international artists, with changing exhibitions throughout the year. Along Sussex Drive is the Royal Canadian Mint, founded in 1908. The Mint offers guided tours. Farther east along Rockcliffe Parkway, but worth the journey, is the Canadian

Spider *Maman*, a 9-metre-tall bronze sculpture by Louise Bourgeois, stands in the National Gallery's plaza.

Aviation and Space Museum. Along with displays of aviation history to the space age, there is the chance to fly in a vintage biplane.

Back in the centre, four floors of discovery await at the Canadian Museum of Nature, where children can explore aspects of the natural world. Galleries are dedicated to prehistoric creatures, mammals, birds, water and more. Northeast of this museum is the Canadian War Museum. Built of mainly recycled materials, including copper from the old Library of Parliament, and sporting a green roof, the museum is a model of eco-design at its best. Art, artifacts and a number of military vehicles make up the museum's displays. Its most poignant piece is the tomb

Byward Market
It's one of the oldest markets in the country and a vibrant shopping district. Stop by to taste some of Ottawa's best food and enjoy the entertainment.

National Arts Centre
See the best of the performing arts from French and English theatre productions and symphony orchestras to ballet and contemporary dance.

Dow's Lake
Depending on the season, rent a boat or some skates, and then have a bite to eat while looking out over the lake.

Rideau The canal freezes in winter, turning the Rideau into the world's longest skating rink—7.2 kilometres from the Parliament Buildings to Dow's Lake.

of an unknown soldier from the First World War, on its own in Memorial Hall. Every November 11th at 11 a.m., the sun shines through the glass and illuminates the stone.

Parliament Hill

The original Parliament Buildings, overlooking the Ottawa River, opened in 1866, just in time for the country's Confederation the following year. Fifty years later, a fire destroyed all of the buildings apart from the Library of Parliament. The beautiful library retains the aura of the early days of Confederation. Its interior of intricately carved pine houses more than 600,000 books and other records. The

City Insider

Words to the wise
Buy a family pass for the museums in the city. Hop aboard a double-decker bus for a tour of the city's main attractions.

Locals love it
The Bytown Museum, in Ottawa's oldest stone building, reveals the rich history of the city and its residents.

How long to stay
A weekend is enough to visit the National Gallery and Parliament Buildings as well as to do some shopping at the market,

but you'll need longer to enjoy the beaches and walk some trails.

What's nearby
Ottawa River, for whitewater rafting; Britannia Beach; Carp, for the Cold War Museum.

When to go
In the winter put on some layers and skate along the Rideau Canal, and take part in the annual Winterlude festival. Be sure to check out the astounding ice sculptures in Confederation Park.

government reconstructed the rest of the Parliament Buildings in the early 1900s. Today's buildings, clad in local limestone, opened for business in 1920, and visitors can watch government in action from galleries above the House of Commons. A link to Ottawa's British past and a ceremonial tradition is the Changing of the Guard on the Hill every morning through the summer. A visit to the Hill is not complete, however, without a trip up the Peace Tower. The tower, named for the men and women who lost their lives in the First World War, is a tall campanile at the front of the Parliament Buildings. An elevator goes to the top of the tower, where there is an observation deck with stunning views of the city and beyond.

Throughout the summer, Parliament Hill is the backdrop for Mosaika, a unique light and sound show that celebrates the diversity of Canada's beautiful landscapes, amazing achievements and what it means to be Canadian. Music and the voices of 200 Canadians fill the air, telling the story in French and English, with accompanying images, lights and visual effects.

Enjoying the Outdoors

Surrounding Ottawa's urban core is a large greenbelt, supplying plenty of room and a variety of terrain for every kind of outdoor activity. Conservation areas, wetlands, forests, golf courses, farms and an equestrian park fill some of the area. Green spaces are everywhere within the city, too, from the groomed parks in the centre to smaller playgrounds. Major's Hill and Confederation are two of the largest urban parks, and both serve as venues for concerts and festivals on Canada Day and throughout the year, such as the Rideau Canal Festival and Winterlude. In June LeBreton Flats Park hosts the International Children's Festival, a celebration of childhood with theatre, art and other activities.

In keeping with the city's affection for outdoor living, more than 220 kilometres of bike trails run through Ottawa. Bike rentals are widely available, so visitors and residents alike can take advantage of this relaxing way to get around. The trails follow the canal and the river, weave through parks and carry cyclists into the main parts of the city. On Sunday mornings throughout the summer, 65 kilometres of parkway are reserved for cyclists, joggers, in-line skaters and other non-motorized travellers.

Friends and Neighbours

Ottawa's proximity to the Gatineau region of Quebec informs a lot of the city's personality. A number of bridges span the river, linking the two provinces of Ontario and Quebec and solidifying Canada's capital city as a true blend of languages and cultures. Don't be surprised if you hear both French and English spoken as you wander the city. The city's official bilingualism is part of its identity and a point of pride.

The city's cultural diversity does not end there. Its residents have flocked to the capital from all over the world and a tour of the city's neighbourhoods reveals its cosmopolitan makeup. Italians settled around Preston Street, the heart of Corso Italia, while Asian immigrants headed just north of here to Somerset Heights. Former villages are now part of the city landscape but retain their own charm and individuality. Westboro is now a trendy neighbourhood, west of Parliament Hill by the river.

A Blaze of Colour

During the Second World War, the Dutch royal family sought refuge in Ottawa. As thanks for Canada's hospitality and the Canadian troops' role in freeing the Netherlands, Princess Juliana presented the city with a gift of 100,000 tulip bulbs. In 1946, she sent another 20,000 bulbs. As a symbol of international friendship, the tradition of giving bulbs has continued every year. Renowned photographer, Malak Karsh, took many photos of the tulips in bloom and suggested a festival with the tulip as its centrepiece. In May 1953 Ottawa held the first Tulip Festival, which has become the largest of its kind in the world. Every spring glorious blooms cloak the city in vivid colour.

fossils. A trip to the Bonnechere Museum will answer all questions about the history of the caves and the area around the Bonnechere River.

The Gatineau Hills are across the Ottawa River, in Quebec. Gatineau Park is the place for camping, hiking, swimming, skiing or simple pleasures such as walks and picnics. Getting to the park is only a short, 15-minute drive from Ottawa, however, it is seemingly a thousand miles from the city's busy urban streets. Nestled in the park, Wakefield is one of the first villages settled along the Gatineau River. Here, historic charm and contemporary vibrancy meet in the numerous galleries, live music venues and festivals. Wakefield's rural setting means that nature is just on the doorstep for wandering the hills or paddling down the river.

Manotick, in the southern part of the city by the Rideau River, retains much of its village appeal. The old gristmill still runs there. Victoria Island has strong ties to the history and tradition of the Algonquin people who consider the island a sacred meeting place. Back on the mainland, New Edinburgh and Rockcliffe are home to the city's grandest residences, including the Prime Minister's home at 24 Sussex Drive and Rideau Hall, the Governor-General's official home since 1867. Rideau Hall is open for public tours of the residence and for its fine art collection.

Daytripping from Ottawa

A short drive in any direction away from the city will lead to somewhere beautiful and interesting to spend a day. South of Ottawa and close in proximity to one another are Smiths Falls, Merrickville and Perth. Smiths Falls and Merrickville, both Loyalist towns, grew up along parts of the Rideau Canal, and their stories are intricately linked with the history of the canal. The Rideau Canal Museum at Smith Falls recounts the tales associated with the canal, its builders and the people who came to depend on it. Perth, on the Tay River in the Rideau Valley, is a parkland village. Its wildlife reserve on Tay Marsh is home to geese, ducks, bluebirds and other wetland creatures.

Travelling northwest of the city is the small community of Eganville. There, visitors can explore the depths of the Bonnechere Caves, where stalactites hang from the ceilings and limestone walls hold thousands of ancient

A Dozen Great Provincial Parks in Ontario

Algonquin Provincial Park

Ontario's first designated provincial park is the ultimate destination for canoeing, fishing, camping and hiking. Algonquin's vast landscape contains more than 1,500 lakes, 1,200 streams and thousands of campsites. Because the park lies within a transitional zone, with deciduous forests to the south and coniferous forests to the north, Algonquin supports a diversity of plant and wildlife, including moose, deer and beaver. An unforgettable Algonquin experience is the annual August wolf howl. This organized, nighttime event leads visitors to a special site to listen quietly while wolves communicate with one another. For keen anglers, Algonquin's pristine waters yield some of the best lake and brook trout available, although catching the best fish may mean a portage into the interior.

For the most authentic Algonquin experience, many people opt to explore the park's trails or backcountry. Brent Crater Trail is a 2-kilometre loop that allows hikers to explore the famous Brent meteorite crater. In the backcountry rustic ranger's cabins offer an alternative to a tent. Either way, rent a canoe before you go so you can paddle along some of the 2,000 kilometres of canoe trails, including in Barron Canyon, and portage through the park's gorgeous scenery. The park is still popular in the autumn when the seasonal change brings a

Other Great Provincial Parks

Bon Echo, Cloyne. Mazinaw Rock rises a steep 100 metres above Mazinaw Lake and dominates the Bon Echo vista. More than 200 aboriginal pictographs adorn the Rock, which is also a magnet for rock climbers.

Bronte Creek, Oakville. Much of this southern Ontario park had once been farmland, and on site is an original, restored homestead and children's play barn. The park holds a maple syrup festival each spring.

Frontenac, Sydenham. This is an all-season playground: winter fun includes ice fishing and snowshoeing, while hiking trails and campsites await summer visitors. The park offers wilderness training.

Inverhuron, Tiverton. This provincial park is an inviting mix of sandy beachfront, lakeside cottages and campsites. Activities include fishing, boating and birdwatching.

Kawartha Highlands, Bancroft. One of Ontario's "Signature Sites," much of Kawartha Highlands remains unspoiled. Located on the southern edge of the Canadian Shield, the park's rock barrens attract numerous birds.

Killarney, Killarney. A wildneress park on the shores of Georgian Bay, this is a dramatically beautiful area distinguished by its white quartzite cliffs. The park's observatory is the perfect spot for stargazing.

Lake Superior, Wawa. This huge, wild park lies along the shore of the largest freshwater lake in the world. It offers stunning views from the Coastal Trail, deep canyons, white water rapids, gushing waterfalls and abundant opportunities for wildlife watching.

Pinery, Grand Bend. Located on the shores off Lake Huron, Pinery offers woodland, sand dunes, hiking and cycling trails and a stunning beach. The park has 1,000 campsites. In the winter the cross-country ski trails are some of the best in the area.

Polar Bear, Cochrane. Moose and polar bears wander the tundra of Ontario's largest park. Primarily a wildlife reserve, access is only by air and visitors need special permission before using the park's landing strips.

Quetico, Atikokan. Early fur traders and Ojibwa hunters paddled the many waterways in what is now Quetico Provincial Park. Even today, park access is primarily by boat and considered a canoeist's paradise.

Sandbanks, Picton. Sandbanks is famous for its giant dunes, some as high as 25 metres. In addition to the beach on Lake Ontario, Sandbanks has many facilities, including campgrounds and canoe rentals.

panorama of brilliant colour, warm days and cooler nights. During the winter months, much of the park is closed or inaccessible, but on-site insulated yurts provide accommodation for up to six people each and may be the best option for a winter visit. If you're not staying in the park, you can take the scenic route along Highway 60, although you will need a park permit to use any of its facilities such as picnic grounds.

Planning: In the busy summer season it's advisable to reserve a campsite, although the park is so big that there are plenty of options if you don't need all the amenities of the developed campgrounds.

Along the Loyalist Highway

KINGSTON

This regal city is home to one of Canada's oldest universities, Queen's, as well as 19th-century limestone buildings and streets lined with stately Victorian homes. Kingston was an important port in the 18th and 19th centuries and retains much of its maritime history. Across from the city centre is Fort Henry, originally built in the 1830s, where you can step back into 19th-century military life. Waterfront parks provide a calm break from the city streets, including Macdonald Park, which runs along Lake Ontario. Nearby is Bellevue House, the former home of Sir John A. Macdonald. Running along the lakeshore is Ontario Street, one of the city's oldest roads. A wander along here leads to the imposing city hall and the Marine Museum of the Great Lakes, where visitors can board the *Alexander Henry*, an old icebreaker. To experience the lake first-hand, head to one of the marinas for sailing, yachting, windsurfing or cruising. A short ferry ride away is Wolfe Island. More than 200 species migrate through the island or nest there, making it ideal for birdwatching.

PLANNING

There are numerous guided tours of the city, including several historical walks. Depending on the season, there are many city events, including music festivals in the summer and FebFest, a citywide winter celebration.

PORT HOPE

British Loyalists settled Port Hope in the late 18th century, and its historic charm is evident. Stroll along the well-preserved main street and go bargain hunting in the many antique stores, or stop at any of the three art galleries; the restored Capitol Theatre is just around the corner. Near the harbour is the Canadian Fire Fighters Museum, open during summer months. The other museum stop in Port Hope is Dorothy's House, a restored worker's cottage. Ganaraska River, which runs through the town, offers anglers salmon and trout fishing.

A little farther east of the city is another former Loyalist settlement: Cobourg. Like Port Hope, Cobourg is a heritage town. The Prince of Wales visited in 1860, officially opening Victoria Hall, which still stands in the city centre. Both Port Hope and Cobourg have beaches and are ideally situated for boating activities. Cobourg's summer Waterfront Festival celebrates Canada Day weekend with a large, open aircraft show and spectacular fireworks over Lake Ontario.

PLANNING

Situated between Toronto and Kingston, Port Hope is an easy day trip from either centre. Summer visits benefit from water activities; an autumn trip could include a day at Port Hope's long-running fall fair.

PRINCE EDWARD

A rural idyll by the lake, Prince Edward County's island community forms one of the loveliest areas in Ontario. Renowned for its lush landscape, wineries, artists, beaches and fine food, the region holds numerous delights for travellers looking for something special. Many people head to

Produce and crafts for sale Kingston Public Market, in historic Springer Market Square, opened in 1801, making it one of Canada's oldest markets.

Impressive lift Built in 1904, Peterborough's Lift Lock in Trent Canal is the highest hydraulic lift lock in the world. The lock lifts boats an average of 19.8 metres.

Reynolds House, in Wellington, dates to 1786 and is one of the oldest homes in Ontario. A great way to see Prince Edward County is by bicycle. Follow the Arts Trail and visit some of the many artists' studios, take in some wineries or enjoy a gourmet tour.

PLANNING
The county is ideal for a weekend escape any time of year or a beach holiday in summer. Countylicious is for food lovers in autumn.
👫 🏛 🚴 🖼 🦅 ⛵

PETERBOROUGH
The city of Peterborough sits on the Trent-Severn Waterway, where summer cruises are popular, especially for those who want to experience the hydraulic lift lock. Other sites include the Canadian Canoe Museum, a unique space that celebrates the country's connection to this watercraft. Peterborough is the centre of the Kawartha Lakes district and surrounded by lush scenery. Not far from the city are lovely towns such as Kawartha Lakes and Fenelon Falls. To get a sense of the area's aboriginal history, visit Petroglyphs Provincial Park. The park's rock faces feature 900 petroglyphs carved hundreds of years ago, and the site itself is sacred to First Nations people. To experience First Nations culture directly, visit Curve Lake First Nation Reserve. The reserve welcomes visitors to learn about the Ojibwa people. Don't miss the Whetung Ojibwa Centre, where you can purchase native crafts and art.

PLANNING
Summertime visits mean a host of outdoor activities. The 4th Line Theatre, near Millbrook, presents works by Canadian playwrights in a beautiful, rural setting.
👫 🏛 🖼 ⛵

Sandbanks Provincial Park for its fabulous beaches, but the county's long shoreline offers abundant opportunities for sailing and swimming. The interior of the county is dotted with little villages that together make up the municipality. If travelling west along the Loyalist Highway from Kingston, you can take the ferry from Glenora across to the islands, and then continue to Picton. Visit Crystal Palace, built around 1887, which is a smaller version of Joseph Paxton's building of the same name in London, and the Regent Theatre, an art deco cinema. The Loyalist Highway continues to wind through the county, passing historic sites along the way.

1,000 Islands

Straddling the border between the United States and Canada are the Thousand Islands of the St. Lawrence River. Boat cruises from Kingston, Gananoque and Brockville tour the islands and include stops at some of the islands' attractions. One of the most impressive is Boldt Castle, on Heart Island in the United States. Wealthy hotelier George C. Boldt built the castle for his wife, but he neither lived in the castle nor returned to the island after she died suddenly in 1904.

Petroglyphs The ancient images in Petroglyphs Provincial Park feature reptiles, shamans, boats and other symbols carved into the marble rock face.

Touring Vibrant Toronto

Canada's largest, most cosmopolitan city has stunning architecture, bustling markets, sprawling parkland and a sparkling waterfront facing Lake Ontario.

Toronto's energy is palpable and contagious. Visitors can feel it as they stroll through the city's markets, move to the music of a summer festival, enjoy a symphony at the Roy Thomson Hall or catch a performance at the Elgin and Winter Garden Theatre Centre, the world's last, operating "double-decker" theatre complex. Outdoors, visitors can tour the city parks, beaches, golf clubs and hiking trails. High Park, in the west end, is Toronto's largest park. Other gems include Riverdale Farm, a rural Ontario farm right in the urban centre. After sunset, there are jazz clubs, nightclubs, theatre and, in winter, nighttime skating at Nathan Phillips Square. Every autumn Nuit Blanche transforms the city into a magical place with an all-night celebration of contemporary art.

Dramatic façade The Royal Ontario Museum houses a collection ranging from dinosaurs to Chinese treasures.

The Habourfront

This area draws visitors and city dwellers alike with lake views and numerous cafés, a dance theatre and craft studios. There's plenty to enjoy, whatever the season. In summer rent a sailboat or even a yacht, or dine by the marina. In winter pull on a pair of ice skates and glide around the Natrel Rink. Year round, the city's largest sports and music venues, the Rogers Centre and the Air Canada Centre, play host to world-class entertainment. While near the lakeshore, continue west and then slightly north to take a step back in time at Fort York. First built in 1793, the fort sits on a famous battle site from the War of 1812. The site contains Canada's largest collection of original, restored 1812 buildings.

Sky Highs

The lakeshore's dominant and most famous feature is also the city's most iconic building: the CN Tower. Enjoy a bite at the tower's revolving restaurant. For the more adventurous, the Edge Walk offers the thrill of a lifetime. Strapped to a harness, walkers navigate the edge of the Tower from 356 metres above the ground and truly experience a bird's-eye view of the city.

Lakeside setting The CN Tower seems to pierce the sky as a ferry plies Lake Ontario in front of Toronto's distinctive and celebrated skyline.

In late summer grounds by the lake turn into an 18-day extravaganza of amusement rides, agricultural and sports exhibits, and entertainment. The Canadian Exhibition, fondly called "the Ex," has run annually for well over a hundred years. On the same site in November the Royal Agricultural Winter Fair settles in for dog shows, a rodeo and the prestigious Royal Horse Show.

Museums for Every Taste

Toronto's many galleries and museums run the gamut from small, focused collections to huge, state-of-the-art exhibitions. Some of the city's more unusual and distinctive museums include: the Bata Shoe Museum, a shoe and history lover's delight; the Gardiner Museum, a showcase of ceramics old and new; and the Design Exchange, celebrating innovative design. The Hockey Hall of Fame pays tribute to Canada's favourite sport. Both a museum and a hall of fame, visitors can enjoy hands-on activities, hockey memorabilia and two theatres.

One of the city's more unusual museums is Casa Loma, Toronto's very own castle set in acres of beautiful gardens. Its existence is the result of one man's dream of building

Don't Miss

Yorkville
Designer boutiques, fine restaurants and fabulous art galleries line the streets. You can relax and people-watch in the urban park.

Dundas Square
A modern outdoor venue for concerts and theatrical events, it is near the city's largest shopping complex, the Eaton Centre.

Toronto Music Garden
This lakeside garden's design was inspired by Bach's *First Suite for Unaccompanied Cello*; each dance movement in the suite is reflected in a different feature.

Kensington Market
Culture, fashion and urban cool combine in narrow streets crammed with stores selling a cornucopia of ethnic foods and vintage finds.

a medieval-style castle in North America. In 1911 the wealthy financier and military man Sir Henry Pellatt commissioned the building of Casa Loma. The castle includes 98 rooms, but some of the areas, such as the swimming pool and bowling alley, were never completed. Unfortunately, financial difficulties forced Sir Henry and his wife to leave Casa Loma after less than ten years. Today, much of the castle has been restored to its former glory, allowing visitors to marvel at the mansion's splendidly furnished interior, roam its secret passageways and inspect the impressive military collections.

Art All Around

Among the city's fabulous art galleries, must-sees are: the Power Plant, which exhibits the best in contemporary art; the Museum of Inuit Art (MIA), southern Canada's only museum dedicated to northern art; and the renowned Art Gallery of Ontario (AGO). Situated in the downtown core, the AGO's collection includes masterpieces of Canadian art, European collections and changing exhibitions from around the world. The AGO's exterior, renovated in 2008, is a striking example of contemporary design by legendary architect Frank Gehry.

Dotted around the city are historic houses, such as Mackenzie House, Colborne Lodge and the Spadina Museum, which provide a glimpse into Toronto's past. In northern Toronto, Black Creek Pioneer Village, a collection of 40 heritage buildings, recreates a 19th-century rural Ontario community.

Neighbourhoods to Explore

Toronto's ethnic mix is one of its greatest attractions. Immigrants settled the city in different areas, and each neighbourhood still maintains its own, unique atmosphere. Even the street signs are bilingual according to the nationality based there. In the west end you can stroll through Little Italy and savour an authentic cannoli with a cup of espresso, while in the east is Greektown, where A Taste of the Danforth happens

Caribbean carnival An explosion of colour and sound hits the streets for three weeks every summer with a lively mix of music, dance, food and art. The annual parade is one of the highlights.

Old and new Built in 1891, the Flatiron Building contrasts the genteel elegance of Old Town with the glass and metal skyscrapers of the Financial District.

every August. In the centre of the city lively Chinatown is a local and sightseer haunt where fresh fish, trinkets and herbal medicine can be found in the area's crowded stores and markets. Another area worth exploring is Little India. The Gerrard India Bazaar is bursting with colour from the many sari stores and steeped in tantalizing aromas from the restaurants.

Southeast of these areas is Old Town. The historic St. Lawrence Market is the site of Toronto's first city hall and features a sumptuous array of produce, pastries and specialty food. A little farther west is the Distillery District with an eclectic mix of cafés, galleries and artisan's studios housed in Victorian industrial buildings. In the same vein West Queen West has overtaken its older sister, Queen West, as the trendy, chic hangout for Toronto's artists and musicians.

Toronto Islands

Escape the urban pleasures for a few hours or a whole day by taking the ferry from Queen's Quay across to the Toronto Islands.

Star Power

The Toronto International Film Festival (TIFF) has emerged as the most important and respected in the circuit after Cannes. Every September the city buzzes with international film stars, directors, producers and first-time filmmakers, all here to promote and celebrate the best in world cinema. The festival features big-budget Hollywood movies, art house films and compelling documentaries. TIFF Bell Lighthouse is the base of the festival, featuring a five-storey complex with five cinemas, two galleries, a film reference library and restaurants.

Chinatown shopping Pick up bargains galore from street vendors, then stop for delicious dim sum.

As you leave, look back for one of the best views of the city skyline. Then get ready to walk or cycle the trails, take a ride on the miniature railway or the antique carousel in Centreville Amusement Park, or simply enjoy a picnic by the water.

This small chain of islands was created by a series of moving sandbars and eroded stone from the Scarborough Bluffs in the east. In the 1800s wealthy Torontonians built summer homes on the islands, and others flocked to enjoy the lakeside beaches and parkland. Today, a small community lives on the islands and take great pride in the car-free, tranquil atmosphere. The islands feature a children's amusement park and small farm, yacht clubs and pools, as well as opportunities to rent bicycles or boats to go exploring. The islands also boast the oldest surviving lighthouse on the Great Lakes, Gibralter Point Lighthouse, and host the Toronto International Dragon Boat Race Festival each year.

A Dozen Great Day Trips from Toronto

Dundas

Here's a destination for those interested in visiting charming towns and also for nature lovers. More than 100 waterfalls cascade over the rocky Niagara Escarpment that runs high above Dundas and the surrounding area. The escarpment's numerous nature trails lead to many of the falls, which vary in style from ribbon to curtain. The Spencer Gorge/Webster's Falls Conservation Area trails near Dundas take hikers to two of the more scenic falls, Tew's Falls and Webster's Falls. Another point of interest in the conservation area is Dundas Peak, a lookout point that offers stunning views of the town and beyond. There is also a concentration of falls between Dundas

and Burlington. A hike along the Bruce Trail provides viewing access to many of these, including Borer's Falls, one of the most popular for sightseers. In the 19th century the area's streams and waterfalls attracted a number of industrialists who built sawmills, paper mills and gristmills along the banks. Crook's Hollow Heritage Trail winds past the remains of old workers' houses and the ruin of an old dam and gristmill before arriving at East Greensville Falls.

Dundas itself is a quaint, provincial place with a delightful main street. Tucked into the valley below the escarpment, the town is a quiet gem belonging to the much larger city of Hamilton, although it maintains

Other Great Day Trips

African Lion Safari, Cambridge. See lions, monkeys and giraffes up close from your car or in a safari bus. Watch an exhibition of birds of prey or see elephants swim and play in the lake. At Pet's Corner there are opportunities to see some smaller or domestic animals.

Belfountain. A drive through the Caledon Hills takes you to this Credit River Valley village. The conservation area is close by. After crossing the suspension bridge, hikers can relax by the historic fountain.

Campbellville. This small village is nestled into the Niagara Escarpment and a pretty river runs through it. The village is dotted with antique stores, and nearby is the Streetcar and Electric Railway Museum, where visitors can take a ride on a restored streetcar.

Canada's Wonderland, Vaughan. A short trip north lands you to this popular amusement park. Good for all ages, Wonderland has hundreds of rides and attractions, a water park and a concert venue.

Glen Williams. Williams Mill Visual Arts Centre is the focal point of this tiny village. The Centre is home to more than 30 studios featuring the work of sculptors, painters, weavers, potters and others.

Hamilton. The city's best attractions lie on the outskirts. Dundurn Castle is a restored 19th-century mansion built in the 1830s by Sir Allan MacNab. The Royal Botanical Gardens, the largest in the country, includes a lovely rock garden and a wildlife sanctuary, Cootes Paradise.

Kleinburg, Vaughan. Just north of Toronto is the cultural haven of Kleinburg. The Humber River runs through this rural town, founded more than 200 years ago. The McMichael Gallery is the main attraction, featuring works by Tom Thomson and the Group of Seven and other artists.

Port Perry. This town northeast of Toronto boasts a marina on Lake Scugog, Victorian architecture and a charming downtown core. Glen Major Forest, east of town, is a treat for hikers and cyclists.

Lake Simcoe. Fishing, boating, swimming and lakefront festivals are some of the area's attractions; away from the water, you can take a ride on the South Simcoe Railway or watch a horserace at Georgian Downs.

Oakville. The upscale city of Oakville, on Lake Ontario, is a heady mix of historic architecture, green space, lakefront and boutique shopping. Glen Abbey, one of Canada's top golf courses is here, too.

Unionville, Markham. Founded more than 200 years ago, many of Unionville's handsome homes and other buildings have been maintained or restored to their original beauty.

a separate identity. Dundas's notable buildings include the Collins Hotel, built in 1841, the Town Hall, built in 1849, and a number of storefronts and residences built in varying architectural styles, including some fine Italianate examples. Dundas is also home to an art school and the Carnegie Art Gallery, housed in the former library building funded by American industrialist Andrew Carnegie.

Planning: Some of the falls go dry during a particularly hot summer, so check before visiting. Springtime is prime viewing time, or travel to the area in winter to see the falls frozen in ribbons of ice.

Wine and Orchard Country

Pastel colours In spring the orchards surrounding Lincoln turn a wonderful shade of pink as peach blossoms fill the fields.

LINCOLN

The town of Lincoln comprises the small towns and hamlets of Beamsville, Jordan, Vineland, Campden and Tintern above and below the Niagara Escarpment. This part of the Niagara region is known for its vineyards, orchards and rolling countryside. In addition to wine tours, roadside fruit stalls, craft cheese makers and antiques stores, there are several conservation areas for hiking, exploration and birdwatching. Part of the Bruce Trail runs through Ball's Falls, an 80-hectare conservation area with hiking trails overlooking Twenty Mile Creek, two waterfalls and a restored 19th-century hamlet, including a flour mill. More rural history and nature waits at the Jordan Historical Museum, which reveals the region's Loyalist and Mennonite roots and features a restored home and schoolhouse. Jordan is also one of the prettiest of Lincoln's villages.

PLANNING
Summer and autumn are the seasons to see the Twenty Valley area at its best. Rent a bicycle to breathe in the scents and appreciate the scenery up close.

ST. CATHARINES
Ontario's "Garden City" is the largest urban area of the Niagara region. It earned its nickname from the many parks, trails and gardens still found around the city. Like many places on Lake Ontario and Lake Erie, Loyalists settled St. Catharines in the late 1700s, but the opening of the Welland Canal established St. Catharines' importance in the area. Remnants of the old canal are dotted around the city. Constructed between 1913 and 1932, the existing canal moves ships up and down the steep escarpment. A visit to the Welland Canals Centre at Lock 3 allows a view of the canal lock in action. Montebello Park, in the heart of the city, hosts summer concerts, and the popular Niagara Wine Festival. On the city's outer limits is Port Dalhousie, a pretty lakeside village with an antique carousel ride near the beach.

PLANNING
The September wine festival is one of St. Catharines' greatest attractions. The summer rowing competition, the Royal Canadian

Lush Vineyards

Niagara's temperate climate and fertile land make it the ideal place for grape growing. Many of the region's wineries produce vintage and award-winning wines, and most offer tours and tastings. Several wineries have full restaurants attached and bus service to nearby accommodations. Niagara is world famous for its icewine, made by harvesting frozen grapes after the first frost. After pressing, the ice rises to the top and leaves a sweet, concentrated juice at the bottom.

Mane attraction The horses and other animals on Port Dalhousie's carousel were all hand carved. The horses still have real horsehair tails.

Henley Regatta, is the largest of its kind in North America and well worth a visit.
🏛 🖼 🕊 🦈 🐦

NIAGARA-ON-THE-LAKE

History is everywhere in Niagara-on-the-Lake. It was the first capital of Ontario, a strategic location during the War of 1812 and the site of Ontario's first library. The town's lakeside golf club opened in 1875, making it the oldest club in North America. Today, the town retains its historic sensibility with refurbished 19th-century buildings, stately homes, museums and monuments, but the mood is also one of relaxation and luxury. Many people come to stroll the town's picturesque streets and shopping districts, and stay in the extended network of cozy inns or at the elegant Prince of Wales Hotel.

History buffs will appreciate visits to the Laura Secord homestead and to Fort George, the British army headquarters during the War of 1812. At the fort costumed staff and volunteers offer insights into the area's history and life inside the fortress.

Other cultural pursuits include the artists and antiques route in and around the town, wine tours and the annual Shaw Festival, which produces works by George Bernard Shaw and his contemporaries. Two of Niagara-on-the-Lake's many open spaces are Queen's Royal Park, with views over Lake Ontario, and Memorial Park, which includes an outdoor pool and playground. A short, scenic drive along the Niagara Escarpment is Queenston Heights, the site of an 1812 battle and now a large park with gardens and green spaces.

PLANNING

The best way to approach Niagara-on-the-Lake is via the Niagara Parkway. The road winds along the Niagara Escarpment, with stunning views over the Niagara River.
🏛 🪑 🖼 🦈

PORT DOVER

Once a busy port town, Port Dover is still known for its marina and fishing and retains the ambiance of a seaside village.

From grapes to wine Niagara has been producing wine for more than 200 years. VQA Ontario labelled wines must be made from Ontario-grown grapes.

A long stretch of sandy beach lies along the northern shore of Lake Erie. The shallow waters make it a good choice for families. The quaint but fascinating Harbour Museum has exhibits detailing the rich history of the area, as well as a dry-docked fishing vessel from the 1930s and hands-on activities. The town's other main attraction is the Lighthouse Festival Theatre, which is housed in the old Town Hall. A journey along the coast of Lake Erie brings you to Long Point Provincial Park, located on a sandspit that juts into the lake. Long Point is a protected wetland that teems with birds and other wildlife.

PLANNING

The town's population doubles in summer when opportunities for water sports abound. There are festivals throughout the year, such as the Polar Bear Plunge on New Year's Day.
👪 🏛 🕊 🦈 🐦

THE WONDER OF NIAGARA

These magnificent Niagara Falls are the most powerful in North America and a breathtaking sight. There are many ways to see them, including a trip on the *Maid of the Mist* to get up close, or a view from above in the Skylon Tower. Every night a stunning array of colours illuminates the falls, creating a magical atmosphere.

Planning:
Aside from the lure of Niagara Falls themselves, there are a number of other attractions, including a marine land, parks and a glitzy casino.

protected natural environment. Unlike many provincial parks, the area has no formal campgrounds and camping is prohibited at several locations. However, this makes the park more attractive to those looking to explore a truly unspoiled part of Ontario. The park is a short drive north from Toronto, but remarkably different from the southern parts of the province. Forested with white pine and black spruce and interspersed with wetlands, lakes, cliffs and falls, the best way to explore the park is by canoe or on foot. Part of the Ganaraska Hiking Trail runs through here. The trail goes from Port Hope and splits north of Lake Simcoe, meeting the Bruce Trail.

PLANNING
Be prepared for rustic conditions. Ganaraska Hiking Trail members have parking privileges at Moore Falls and Victoria Bridge.

Cottage Country

HALIBURTON
Ancient rocks of the Canadian Shield and soaring trees surround the roads that wind in and around the Haliburton Highlands. In the warmer months canoeists and kayakers tour the county's many water trails that weave through lakes and along rivers. The hundreds of lakes offer spectacular fishing opportunities year-round for northern pike, muskies and rainbow trout. Hikers get spectacular views of the county from various lookout points along the many trails. Haliburton doesn't stop in winter, with open trails for snowmobiling, cross-country skiing and snowshoeing.

In addition to its outdoor appeal, the region has a well-established reputation as an artisans' community. One of the Highland's nature trails rambles through the lovely Haliburton Sculpture Forest, near the town. Many artists live here year-round and open their studios during the annual tour every autumn. A little off the beaten track, and definitely out of the ordinary, is the Highlands Cinemas in Kinmount. As well as showing first-run films, the cinema showcases movie memorabilia.

PLANNING
Haliburton is a year-round destination for the outdoor enthusiast; brilliant foliage colours makes a trip in autumn worthwhile.

QUEEN ELIZABETH II
Situated between the cottage areas of Haliburton and Muskoka is Queen Elizabeth II Wildlands Provincial Park, a huge,

MUSKOKA
The town of Gravenhurst is a gateway to reach the beautiful, rugged Muskoka region to the north. The lumber industry brought development and settlers to Gravenhurst. Medical pioneer Norman Bethune was born in the town, and his family home is now a museum. Today, the region is a popular playground for the wealthy and famous, even earning the nickname "Millionaire's Row" for a stretch of mansions along Lake Muskoka. Lake Joseph and Lake Rousseau are the other large lakes in the area; there are 1,600 lakes altogether for canoeing, sailing, fishing and swimming.

Port Carling, a small but pretty town on the Indian River, is in the centre of Muskoka. The town's central location, antique shops, boutiques and restaurants make it a hotspot for visitors. Huntsville lies in the northeast

Sainte-Marie among the Hurons

Before the arrival of French explorers and settlers, the Huron people lived on the land around Georgian Bay. French Jesuits arrived in the 17th century and built a mission there. The Jesuits and Hurons lived together peacefully for ten years until the attacking Iroquois forced them to abandon the mission. Today, Sainte-Marie among the Hurons is a reconstruction of the mission as it was in the times of the Jesuits. Activities include aboriginal storytelling in the reconstructed longhouse and a celebration of Canada's National Aboriginal Day in June.

corner of Muskoka, near Algonquin Park. The town is the last, major stop before the park and is the best place to pick up canoe rentals and essentials. It's also a place for exploring. Hop onboard the *Portage Flyer*, a vintage train ride at Muskoka Heritage Place, or take in a show at the Algonquin Theatre. Arrowhead Provincial Park, just north of

the town, is ideal for a wilderness escape. Muskoka's eastern border town is Dorset, in the Lake of Bays. A climb up the Scenic Lookout Tower offers amazing, 360-degree views from 146 metres in the sky.

PLANNING

The summer is peak tourist season, but there are many campsites, resorts and cottage rentals available and numerous activities to fill the long, light-filled summer days.

MIDLAND

Huronia's largest town is Midland, on the southern shores of Georgian Bay. The town is small, but it packs in a number of attractions, including Wye Marsh, a bird-lover's paradise. Boardwalks, hiking and skiing trails surround this wetland wildlife centre. An observation tower provides a quiet spot for wildlife watching. The community's aboriginal story comes to life at the Huronia Museum and Huron/Ouendat Village. The reconstruction looks at life in the 1500s, before the Europeans arrived. Sainte-Marie among the Hurons is also worth a visit (see above left).

Mission of peace The spires of the Martyr's Shrine Church, Midland, rise above the reconstructed Jesuit mission of Sainte-Marie among the Hurons.

Just north of Midland, is Penetanguishene, a bilingual town on the site of an old British naval base. The Discovery Harbour site reconstructs the dockyards and buildings of the base. Farther north are the cobble and sand beaches of Awenda Provincial Park, while Georgian Bay Islands National Park is a mix of rocky outcrops, forests and wetlands. Lighthouses dot the landscape around the bay. The Christian Island lighthouse, first used in 1859, is the oldest. Cruises leave from both Midland and Penetanguishene to tour some of Georgian Bay's thousands of islands.

PLANNING

Visit in summer to enjoy all of the area's attractions, including boat cruises that are not available in the winter months.

Surrounded by water Muskoka's clear lakes and rivers are the perfect choice for kayaking, with rapids providing an extra thrill.

Moving West

ELORA

When Scottish settlers chose Elora to set down roots, they were more interested in the power that the Grand River could provide their mills than the striking beauty of the Elora Gorge. Today, Elora is home to many artists, writers and craftspeople drawn to the town's stunning setting and laid-back pace. Small, independent stores, cafés and an art house cinema have taken over the old buildings that line Mill Street and Geddes Street. Away from the commercial part of town, the peaceful and pretty residential streets lead to Victoria Park and a walking trail that skirts the cliff tops and provides views over the gorge. Just outside of town is the Elora Conservation Area, where canoeists, tubers and kayakers can take on the white rapids for an exhilarating ride. For swimmers, there is the Elora Quarry, which features a beach in an old, limestone quarry surrounded by cliffs. A short drive down a country road takes you to the Wellington County Museum, a former poor house that now holds artists' workshops and contemporary art exhibits as well as displaying area archives.

PLANNING

Summer is the height of the tourist season, but Elora is also charming in the spring and autumn. The annual arts festival in summer and studio tours are highlights of the year.

CRAWFORD LAKE

The gorgeous Crawford Lake and its conservation lands lie atop the Niagara Escarpment, near Milton. The lake is a rare, meromictic body of water, meaning that its layers do not mix. As a result, archaeologists were able to dig into the undisturbed lake bottom and study the sediment. These studies led to information about the Iroquois people who lived there centuries ago. A meticulously reconstructed, 15th-century Iroquoian village now stands near the lake and features longhouses and gardens. To preserve the vulnerable condition of the lake, but enable visitors to enjoy its beauty, an elevated boardwalk surrounds it. Walking trails wind through the forested area and connect to Rattlesnake Point, another area of natural beauty. The Bruce Trail, Canada's oldest and longest hiking path, which runs 885 kilometres along the length of the escarpment, traverses Crawford Lake Conservation Area.

PLANNING

The conservation area is open year-round for snowshoeing and cross-country skiing in the winter and hiking in summer. The melting snow in spring signals the arrival of maple syrup and the accompanying, annual festival that celebrates the "sweet water season."

STRATFORD

Although famous for its Shakespearean festival (see right), Stratford's delights do not end there. Situated along the lovely Avon River, complete with swans, Stratford is a 19th-century architectural gem with a vibrant arts community. The city was designated as a Victorian Heritage District in 1998, and elegant homes line its streets. Stratford

Frozen in time The furnished longhouse at Crawford Lake includes a fire pit, around which traditional circle gathering and storytelling would take place.

Stratford Shakespeare Festival

The annual Stratford Shakespeare Festival, which runs from April through November every year, has entertained millions of people since Sir Alec Guinness starred in the inaugural performance of *Richard III* in 1953. Now a celebrated and established festival with four theatres, the program features a host of the Bard's plays in addition to works by other great playwrights such as Eugene O'Neill, Henrik Ibsen and Tennessee Williams.

is easy to walk and has self-guided tours. Historic landmarks include the impressive city hall and courthouse. The Mill Block, built on a natural cliff, is the oldest business district and now a boutique-shopping and dining area. The city has several gardens for a tranquil stroll, including The Shakespearean Gardens, awash with fragrant flowers, herb and rose beds. The gardeners chose the plants from those cited in Shakespeare's plays. There is much to do in Stratford itself, but a short drive in the countryside will take you to the heritage village of St. Marys, with

its old limestone quarry—now Canada's largest outdoor swimming pool, and the Canadian Baseball Hall of Fame. If you just can't get enough theatre, the tiny town of Blyth hosts an annual festival that celebrates works by Canadian authors.

PLANNING

The festival season is its busiest, but the city dresses up year-round for crisp autumn or winter walks, cozy fireside dinners, gallery visits and nights at the symphony.

LONDON

Like its British namesake, the Thames River intersects the city of London, Ontario, the largest urban centre in southwestern Ontario. The river plays an important part in London's character. Walking and cycling trails follow the waterway on both sides, and there are numerous spots for canoeing and rowing. The city has more than 200 parks, woodlands and meadows, as well as the

spacious campus of the University of Western Ontario in the city centre. Richmond Row is good for retail therapy, as is the refurbished Covent Garden Market, which first opened in 1845. London's lively music scene draws worldwide talent to the large John Labatt Centre, the London Music Hall and smaller venues. Folk music aficionados descend on the city for the Home County Folk Festival, when musicians and a huge craft show take over downtown's Victoria Park. For families with younger children, Storybook Gardens is the perfect place to spend an afternoon. The themed gardens feature play areas, rides, a small farm, pond and forest. In the winter visitors explore the gardens along the meandering skating trail. Other family-friendly entertainment includes Fanshawe Pioneer Village and a chance to stand inside a reconstructed Iroquoian longhouse at the Museum of Ontario Archaeology.

PLANNING

London fully embraces the winter season. There are hockey games to watch, outdoor skating rinks to enjoy, and cross-country skiing in the Fanshawe Conservation Area.

Bustling market London's Covent Garden Market has been a central gathering place since the mid-1800s. A new building opened in 1999 on the same site.

EXPLORING
MENNONITE
COUNTRY

St. Jacobs is a small, but lively place where old meets new. Rolling farmland surrounds the village, much of it tended by Old Order Mennonites. Mennonites are a familiar sight in St. Jacobs, where they come to sell finely sewn quilts, handmade furniture and fresh produce at the market and in the local stores.

Planning:
Go anytime from spring through autumn to shop at the market. The Elmira Maple Syrup Festival, held for one day in spring, is one of the best in the area.

On the Shores of the Great Lakes

GRAND BEND

Campers flock to the shores of Lake Huron in summer and many cite Pinery Provincial Park as their favourite place to stay. The nearby town, Grand Bend, is just as popular in the summer. The north beach is a hotspot for young sun seekers, while families favour the waters by the south beach. Away from the beach, there's golfing at one of the resorts or antique hunting at the two markets, which are treasure troves for bargain hunters. If daytime pursuits are not enough, head to the restaurants and bars that light up Main Street after dark as clubbers fill the dance floors. Behind the Lambton County Heritage Museum are fields once known as Old Thedford Bog. Here is one of Grand Bend's lesser known pleasures—a chance to see thousands of tundra swans as they stop on their way north to the Canadian Arctic.

PLANNING

Summer is the busiest time and popular with a younger crowd. Go in March to see the tundra swans before they leave the area.

🌲 👫 🏛 🛷 🦢 ⛵ 🎣

GODERICH

According to lore, Queen Victoria called Goderich "the prettiest town in Canada," and the label stuck. The beaches, gardens and architecture all add to the gentile atmosphere and beauty of the town. Goderich's main streets emanate from a central square. Among the town's landmarks are: Huron County Museum, which focuses on the region's early development; the Marine Museum, by the lakefront; and the Sky Gallery, dedicated to the history of the airport founded in 1938. Goderich's importance as a regional centre is evident at the Huron Historic Gaol and Governor's House. The former jail operated from 1841 until 1972 within the walls of a forbidding, octagonal-shaped building. One of its inmates was James Donnelly of Lucan's infamous Black Donnellys. To appreciate Goderich's natural beauty, amble along the

A day at the beach Goderich's three sandy beaches are within a short distance of downtown. The beaches have several picnic areas and playgrounds.

Surf's up Crashing waves make Grand Bend popular with surfers, while the brilliant sunsets over Lake Huron are equally inviting.

Lakeside Charm

The small town of Bayfield, just south of its more famous neighbour Goderich, attracts thousands of visitors each year to its tree-lined streets. The town's shopping district is packed with boutiques, and its marina is ideal for renting a boat for an outing on the lake. The Folmar Windmill, modelled after the Dutch Arend windmill, is a working sawmill and gristmill. Visitors can tour the inside.

Marine Walk boardwalk, which skirts the three beaches along Lake Huron, or hike the Goderich to Auburn Rail Trail (G.A.R.T.).

PLANNING
Grab a map of Huron County's numerous, skiing trails to explore in winter.

SOUTHAMPTON

French missionaries and fur traders were among the first Europeans in this area of Bruce County, joining the First Nation Chippewa established along the Saugeen River. Later, British founders called their lakeside settlement Southampton, after the seaport in England. Today, along with Port Elgin and Saugeen Township, Southampton is part of the Town of Saugeen Shores, and sightseers flock to the area for its attractions. South from Port Elgin, unspoiled beachfront wraps the shore, ending at MacGregor Point Provincial Park, a haven for wetlands wildlife. The city of Southampton has a number of cultural highlights. The Southampton Art School, one of the oldest in Ontario, opened its gallery in 1999. Bruce County Museum, overlooking Fairy Lake, has a fine collection of artifacts and is a venue for events and concerts. Just north of Southampton is the Saugeen First Nation amphitheatre, a limestone-encased, outdoor theatre.

PLANNING
In the summer, take a tour to Chantry Island, visit the Keeper's Cottage and take in the view from the Imperial Lighthouse.

TOBERMORY

Surrounded by water on three sides, the town of Tobermory lies at the tip of the Bruce Peninsula. Sailboats and yachts line the docks at its twin harbours, Little Tub and Big Tub, and the town is a jumping-off point for water activities. The waters surrounding the point are favoured by deep-sea anglers fishing for trout, bass and pike. A short boat ride away is Flowerpot Island, famed for its pillars, wild orchids and as a great spot for hiking and camping. The island is part of Fathom Five National Marine Park, the site of several shipwrecks. Glass-bottomed boats allow viewing of the wrecks from above, but scuba divers get a better look. Just outside of Tobermory is the Bruce Peninsula National Park, a rugged area of cliffs, forests and lakes offering camping, canoeing and swimming. Singing Sands Beach, named for the wind that whistles through the sand dunes, is a large beach along the Lake Huron side of the park. Its shallow waters are good for younger children. The Bruce Trail, Canada's longest and oldest path, runs through the park and ends at Tobermory.

PLANNING
Rent scuba diving equipment in the town to experience amazing freshwater diving.

Tobermory Lake waters pounded Flowerpot Island and created the rocky sea stacks seen today. Only two pillars remain since the third stack collapsed in 1903.

BEACH FUN AT WASAGA

The white, sandy shoreline of Wasaga stretches along 14 kilometres of Nottawasaga Bay, Lake Huron, to form the world's longest freshwater beach. Water sports are popular, and the vast expanse of the bay allows for a wide variety. A provincial park protects the area and includes nature and biking trails.

Planning:
The main beach is dotted with umbrellas and sun seekers, but farther along are quieter spots. In the winter nearby Collingwood is a popular ski resort.

Southwestern Ontario

CHATHAM

Farmland surrounds the town of Chatham, where seasonal fruits and vegetables fill the roadside stalls. Situated between Lake St. Claire and Lake Erie, ample opportunities exist for outdoor activities; the beaches and hiking trails of Rondeau Provincial Park are just south of the town. Chatham itself is an older Ontario town by the Thames River, where the ghost tour is a popular way to explore after dark. Tecumseh, a Shawnee chief, died during the Battle of the Thames in 1813 and local legends maintain that his ghost wanders the area. Thousands of car buffs come to Chatham-Kent to attend the region's prestigious auto shows. RetroFest and Old Autos Car Show at Bothwell feature vintage cars, and WAMBO (Wallaceburg Antique Motor and Boat Outing) is one of the largest transportation shows in the country, with antique boats, airplanes, fire trucks and motorcycles on display. Take a short drive north of Chatham to see the Uncle Tom's Cabin Historic Site in Dresden. The home belonged to Josiah Henson, an escaped slave who established a settlement as a refuge for slaves from south of the border. The character in Harriet Beecher Stowe's novel of the same name was based on Henson.

PLANNING

For any outdoor activities, the Chatham area is a pleasure year-round. Car shows happen throughout the summer months.

🌲 👫 🏛 ⛵ 🐟

POINT PELEE

One of Canada's smallest national parks, Point Pelee National Park is a microcosm of amazing plant and animal life. The marshes, fields and forests are home to reptiles, birds and insects found nowhere else in Canada, and the forest features more than 70 species of tree. The park is known as one of the best birdwatching sites in the country, with more than 370 species recorded. The area is an important migration stop for a number of birds and the best place to see the monarch butterfly as it rests briefly before continuing

Wetland haven Point Pelee's Marsh Boardwalk stretches a kilometre across marshlands that are home to turtles, frogs and other wetland creatures.

its epic journey. Point Pelee, the southern, sandy tip of mainland Canada, features the Marsh Boardwalk and observation tower, where visitors may spot an Iceland gull. Jack Miner's Bird Sanctuary is just west of the park. Miner founded the sanctuary in 1904 because he saw geese and ducks stopping to rest at the pond. As more waterfowl arrived, Miner began banding the migrating birds and drew attention to his conservation efforts. In

Finding refuge Uncle Tom's Cabin Historic Site recreates the Dawn Settlement for fugitive slaves. Josiah Henson's home has been restored to its 1850s period.

Pelee Island

About 300 people permanently reside on Pelee Island, but thousands come to the area by ferry to relax on the beaches, hike the island's trails and observe birds. The island is home to the oldest estate winery in Canada and a kite museum. Just south is Middle Island, an uninhabited island officially part of Point Pelee National Park, and Canada's most southerly point.

1918, partly due to the efforts of "Wild Goose Jack," the government designated Point Pelee as a national park.

PLANNING
The first few weeks of May is spring migration time; in autumn look out for birds of prey such as hawks. The visitor's centre has lists of arrival and departure times for bird species.

AMHERSTBURG

Like other towns along the southern Ontario border, Amherstburg was an important place during the War of 1812. King's Navy Yard Park, once a shipyard, is now a waterfront green space where visitors can watch marine re-enactments. When exploring the town, look for "Voices of Amherstburg" signs and activate the guided tour on your cell phone. The town and its surrounding area played a significant part in the Underground Railroad and were a refuge for people escaping slavery in the United States. The North American Black Historical Museum focuses on the Underground Railroad and the Black Canadian history. Attached to the museum is the Taylor Log Cabin, the home of escaped slave George Taylor in the 1880s.

Today, Amherstburg is a destination for a myriad of activities and interests. In addition to its historic appeal, downtown Amherstburg is an enjoyable place to wander

around for its galleries and boutiques. The Gibson Gallery is well worth a visit. South of the city streets are several beaches for swimming, boating and fishing on Lake Erie.

PLANNING
During the summer, take a cruise to and from Windsor; in autumn go to the Hawk Festival at nearby Holiday Beach Conservation Area.

WINDSOR

The French first settled in the area in the 1700s, but the British established Windsor's urban centre. The arrival of the railway, and later the automobile industry, were responsible for the city's reputation as an industrial centre. Industrialists built large homes along the Detroit River, overlooking Detroit, Michigan, across the border. Also on the waterfront is the Art Gallery of Windsor, a large, modern space with one of the best collections of Canadian art in Ontario, and Odette Sculpture Park, an outdoor exhibit of large pieces. The Peace Fountain in Coventry Gardens—the only standalone, floating fountain in the world—sends jets of water 21 metres high. Another gallery must-see is the Canada South Science City, an interactive learning centre with changing exhibits. Windsor's other claim to fame is as the birthplace of Canadian Club rye whisky. Hiram Walker started his distillery in Detroit, but moved it to Windsor, and the Walkerville community developed around it. During Prohibition, Windsor smugglers were a supply source for gangsters such as Al Capone.

PLANNING
A fantastic light show illuminates the Peace Fountain in summer. Visit the Canadian Club Brand Center for a tour and whisky samples.

Setting for an alliance Fort Malden, in Amherstburg, was a British military fortress. Here, Chief Tecumseh and General Brock formed their famous alliance during the War of 1812.

Sculpted rocks Glaciers scraped and eroded the rocks' surface, smoothing and exposing the bedrock that juts out along the French River.

Gateway to the North

PARRY SOUND

Named for Sir William Edward Parry, the Arctic explorer, Parry Sound sits in a harbour on Georgian Bay, just west of Muskoka cottage country. It's the hometown of hockey legend Bobby Orr, and fans will not want to miss the Bobby Orr Hall of Fame that charts Orr's life from humble beginnings to hockey star. The town's location makes it a pleasant layover when exploring the region's natural beauty. A lookout tower in the town awards dramatic views of the bay and its islands and is likely to inspire a tour on one of the cruise ships. The ships leave the harbour

Mattawa

Northern Ontario's past comes to life in Mattawa, a historic town built at the meeting point of the Mattawa and Ottawa rivers, hence the town's name, which means "meeting of the waters" in Ojibwa. The Hudson's Bay Company established a fur-trading post at Mattawa in the 1830s, recognizing the town's importance as a trading centre. The Voyageurs Days Festival in the summer celebrates Mattawa's connections to the French explorers.

in Parry Sound for excursions around the 30,000 islands of Georgian Bay. Killbear Provincial Park lies in the middle of the islands and has campsites for those who would like to stay a little longer. The United Nations has designated this spectacular archipelago of rock and forest as a biosphere reserve. On land the area's topography lends itself to an array of golf courses and resorts, all within magnificent settings.

PLANNING

Festival of the Sound is a classical music summer extravaganza held by the waterfront. 🌲 🏛 ⛵

FRENCH RIVER

Connecting Lake Nipissing to northern Georgian Bay, the French River flows for 105 kilometres through interconnecting lakes, marshes, rapids and falls. The river provided a convenient trading route for the Ojibwa Nation, and French voyageurs used the river as a shortcut for transporting and trading fur. When the fur trade ended the logging industry took over. Some small villages grew up along or near the river, and these provide travellers with essentials when touring the region. Most people come to canoe or kayak parts of the river and enjoy the surrounding scenery. The French River Voyageur Canoe Race, held every year, attracts enthusiastic paddlers. North of French River is another Georgian Bay provincial park, Killarney. One of the oldest European communities here is the village of Killarney, established in 1820.

PLANNING
Stop at the French River Visitor's Centre to view the French River gorge and for a fascinating history on the area.

NORTH BAY
The city of North Bay is the gateway to Ontario's vast northern territory. The city is north of Algonquin Park and a busy urban centre between Lake Nipissing and Trout Lake. Originally a strategic stop on the canoe route and an early fur-trading centre,

North Bay's community grew after the arrival of the railway and as the lumber industry prospered. The city's heritage museum, Discovery North Bay, features information on the city's past. North Bay is famous as the birthplace of the Dionne Quintuplets born in May 1934, and their former home is now a museum. The lakes outside of the city have their own attractions. On Lake Nipissing, nestled in a sheltered bay, is Callander, a quiet but scenic town with lovely beaches. The other side of the lake, around West Nipissing, is a popular hunting ground.

PLANNING
In winter Lake Nipissing is the place for ice fishing. Shuttles are available to heated ice huts that can be rented by the day or longer.

Canoe routes Canoeing on the lake or along traditional routes is a typical North Bay pastime. First Nations hunters introduced Europeans to the routes.

Lake Nipissing West Nipissing's picturesque setting on the lake makes it an enviable holiday destination. The serene lake is ideal for swimming and boating.

TEMAGAMI
The lakes and islands provide fine wilderness escapes in Temagami, and the area's fishing is a prime attraction. There are two provincial parks near Temagami: Marten River and Finlayson Point. A replica, 19th-century logging camp in Marten River Provincial Park brings the area's past to life. Finlayson Point embraces Lady Evelyn-Smoothwater, a vast wilderness park with old-growth pine trees. The town of Temagami has few sights, but local artists display their work at various venues. Nearby is White Bear Forest, where hikers can follow ancient trails.

PLANNING
Climb to the cupola of Temagami's Fire Tower for views of Finlayson Provincial Park.

Northern Ontario

MANITOULIN ISLAND

Situated in the clear waters of Lake Huron, Manitoulin is the world's largest freshwater island. Most people travel to Manitoulin for outdoor activities such as hiking, horseback riding and fishing. The island is dotted with nature reserves, small villages and more than a hundred small lakes. Access to the island is via the swing bridge connecting Manitoulin at its northern point, by plane to one of two airports or by ferry from the south. As a northern section of the Niagara Escarpment, Manitoulin's geography includes rocky cliffs overlooking the lake. The Cup and Saucer Trail, just west of Little Current, is a 14-kilometre path that skirts the cliffs. Many of the island's residents belong to First Nations bands. The Wikwemikong Indian Reserve is unceded, so no treaty was ever signed. The reserve welcomes tourists to its aboriginal theatre and large, annual cultural festival. Within the lands of the M'Chigeeng First Nation, on the northern side of the island, is the Great Spirit Circle Trail, passing by Bear Caves and Fossil Rock Point. The island's European heritage is celebrated in a number of small museums, including the Pioneer Museum in Mindemoya.

PLANNING

Before setting off on a fishing or hunting trip, contact the Ministry of Natural Resources for information on licenses and seasonal limits. 🌲 🦌

SUDBURY

A huge nickel monument greets visitors to one of Sudbury's best attractions, Dynamic Earth. In keeping with the city's mining heritage, visitors to the museum can descend to the Vale Chasm to witness a simulated dynamite blast or step inside a replica of the Fénix 2 capsule used to rescue the Chilean miners. This earth sciences

Monumental coin The Big Nickel is a 10-metre high monument to Sudbury's proud mining heritage and its famous natural resource.

museum is part of the impressive Science North, one of Canada's largest science centres. Science North includes a digital planetarium, IMAX theatre and exhibit space. The Festival of Lights takes place on the museum grounds during winter. Many other festivals take place during the year, such as La fête de la Saint-Jean-Baptiste, a celebration of Sudbury's vibrant francophone community. The Northern Ontario Railroad Museum and Heritage Centre, featuring a mountain steam locomotive, provides an insightful look at the city's mining past and the importance of the railway to the

Artists' Canyon

The paintings of the Group of Seven first brought people's attention to the wild beauty of Agawa Canyon. The artists rented a boxcar to get to the canyon, and the train is still the easiest way to get there, although there are hiking trails for the more energetic traveller. The train tour goes along the top of the canyon and then descends more than 150 metres to its floor. In winter the train travels through a breathtaking, frosted landscape.

Spiritual island Named after the great spirit Manitou, the island is sacred to the Anishnawbe, who lead visitors on the Great Spirit Circle Trail on Manitoulin Island.

northern communities. Trains navigated the lakes, forests and wetlands typical of the geography of the Canadian Shield. Much of that territory remains unspoiled, and several conservation areas are accessible from the city centre, including Fielding Bird Sanctuary, Maley Conservation Area and Lake Laurentian Conservation Area. North of the city is another mining centre, Timmins, a former gold-rush town most famous as the hometown of Shania Twain.

PLANNING

For a northern experience, be a musher for a day and take part in a dogsled adventure.

🌲 👫 🏛 🦅

SAULT STE. MARIE

Known colloquially as "the Soo," this northern Ontario city is one of the oldest European settlements in Canada. Sault Ste. Marie developed along the northern side of St. Marys River, between Lake Huron and Lake Superior. The area is a busy transportation channel between the lakes, but large ships use the American locks and recreational traffic passes through the Canadian locks on the Sault Ste. Marie Canal. The city's scenic boardwalk runs along the river, past the marina and Roberta Bondar Park, an outdoor festival venue. Other attractions within the city include the Canadian Bushplane Heritage Centre, a waterfront hanger that houses 30 aircraft. In the summer swimmers and windsurfers head to Point Des Chenes, a local beach just outside the city centre. Biking opportunities are numerous within and outside of the city. Hiawatha Highlands is a maze of mountain trails for leisurely or more rigorous biking. The Bellevue Valley Trail system runs up along streams and into the hardwood forest

Northern falls Hike along the gorge trails of Kakabeka Falls Provincial Park for spectacular views of the falls, known as the "Niagara of the North."

overlooking Lake Superior. For cross-country skiing, Stokely Creek's trails are some of the best in the country.

PLANNING

Take a helicopter sightseeing tour over the Sault. In February take part in the Bon Soo, northern Ontario's largest winter carnival.

🌲 👫 🏛 ⛷ ⛵ 🦅

THUNDER BAY

Natural wonders abound around the northern shore of Lake Superior. Thunder Bay is the area's largest city and the gateway to many of these spectacular sights. One of these is the rocky, forested peninsula that comprises Sleeping Giant Provincial Park, a hiker's paradise. Canada's longest suspension bridge spans 183 metres over Eagle Canyon, 46 metres above the canyon

floor. Hiking trails surround the canyon, but a thrilling alternative is zip lining to the bottom. The best lookout point is Mount McKay, with views over the city and lake. West of Thunder Bay is Kakabeka Falls, where water cascades from 40 metres high. Fossils of 1.6 billion years old have been unearthed from the rock beneath the falls.

To experience mining first hand, visit the Amethyst Mine Panorama. Novice miners can dig for their own amethyst to keep. Fort William Historical Park, built on the site of a former fur-trading post, is also an impressive attraction. Historical re-enactments, festivals and activities bring its fur-trading past to life.

PLANNING

Spring is the time to visit Kakabeka Falls, when the falls are more forceful.

🌲 👫 🏛

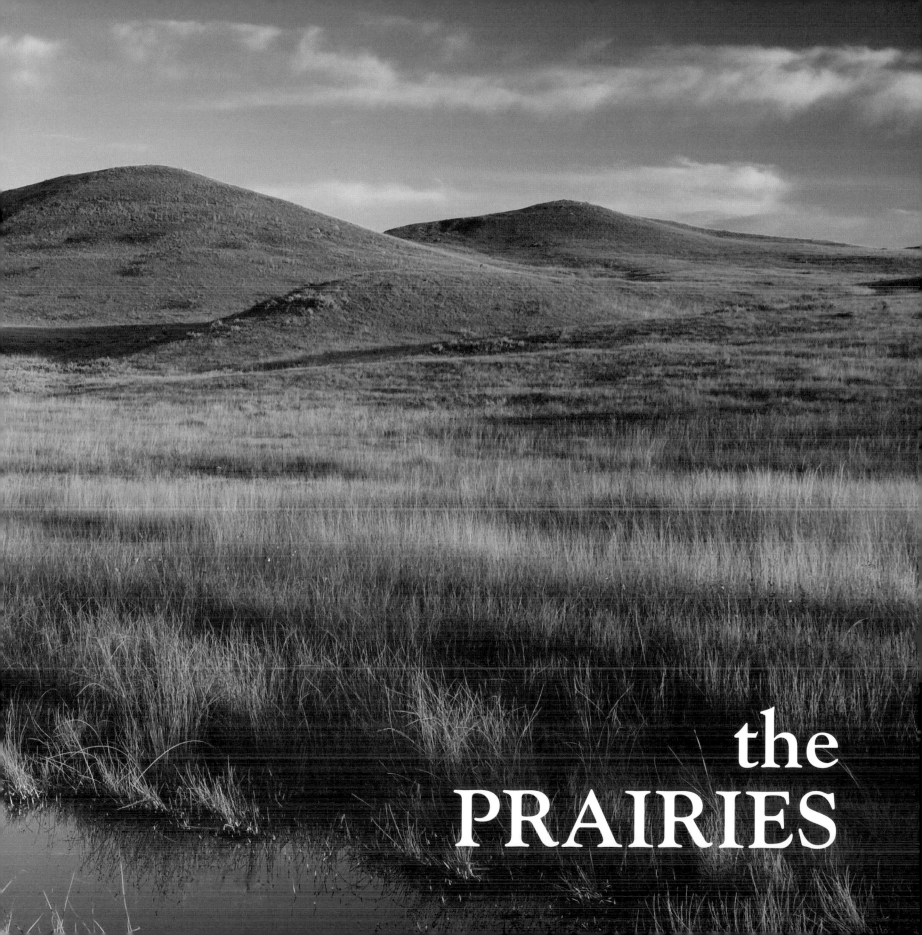

the
PRAIRIES

Discover Winnipeg

Manitoba's metropolis is one of the most surprising of Canada's cities. It is a big, husky prairie town with a mixture of both enterprise and the arts.

Replete with railway yards, factories and a frenetic commodities exchange, Winnipeg also flaunts a sophisticated side that encompasses top-notch cuisine, impressive art galleries and world-class performing arts,

Torch bearer Golden Boy crowns the dome of the Manitoba Legislative Building in downtown Winnipeg.

including theatre, ballet and music, earning it the title "cultural cradle of Canada."

Situated at the confluence of the Assiniboine and Red rivers, the area was first settled by French explorer and fur trader Sieur de La Vérendrye in 1738. After years as a Hudson's Bay Company town, Winnipeg came into its own in the 1870s as capital of the recently created Manitoba province. This "Gateway to the Prairies" has attracted a steady stream of immigrants for two centuries. Many of them went no farther, endowing Winnipeg with a cultural and ethnic mix that includes Anglo-Irish, French, Ukrainian, Polish, Italian, Chinese and Eastern European Jews.

Diverse Downtown

It may have been eclipsed in height by downtown's skyscrapers, but the Manitoba Legislative Building remains the city's most impressive structure. The towering neoclassical landmark was christened in 1920 on the 50th anniversary of the province. Among its noteworthy features are a 72-metre-high dome crowned by the celebrated statue of Golden Boy (officially entitled "Eternal Youth") by French sculptor Georges Gardet, a grand staircase flanked by bronze bison statues and a magnificent, cathedral-like rotunda.

Majestic herd Among the Manitoba Museum's many trademark features is a lifelike diorama of a Métis buffalo hunt, which can be seen in the Orientation Gallery.

Tours of the building are available during the summer. At the southeast corner of the gardens is the Victoria-style Government House, which is the official home of the queen's representative in Manitoba.

An even more inspiring Victorian structure is the Queen Anne Revival-style Dalnavert House, a national historic site that reflects both the design and the mindset of the late 1800s. The lavishly decorated home was built in 1895 as the residence of Sir Hugh John Macdonald, Manitoba's premier and son of Canada's first prime minister. As well

Don't Miss

Assiniboine Park
One of Canada's largest inner city green spaces, the riverside park is home to Winnipeg's zoo, the Pavilion Gallery art museum, an indoor botanical garden, a miniature steam train and trails that are intriguing in every season.

FortWhyte Alive
Perched on the city's southwest edge, this cutting-edge nature centre provides wildlife viewing, environmental education and outdoor recreation that ranges from summer hiking and biking to winter snowshoeing, sledding and lake skating.

Old Market Square
This diminutive park in the Exchange District is the focus of free events for Winnipeg's jazz, folk and fringe festivals and the jumping-off point for numerous historic walking tours. Arrayed around the square are bars, bookstores and the Cinematheque, an avant-garde cinema.

as guided tours, the visitor centre organizes special events throughout the year.

On the north side of Memorial Provincial Park lies the wedge-shaped Winnipeg Art Gallery (WAG). Among its hallmarks are the Gort Collection of medieval and renaissance paintings and tapestries, ceramics and glass from around the world, and a superb assemblage of Canadian and Inuit artworks. Designed by local architect Gustavo da Roza, the building itself is a modern piece of art.

Centennial Square
Winnipeg's cultural hub is Centennial Square, located in the busy Exchange District. One of its prime occupants is the Manitoba Museum, home of one of

City Insider

Words to the wise
Bring your walking shoes. Winnipeg is a pedestrian-friendly city with many guided walking tours on offer.

Locals love it
Winnipeg Jets professional hockey team, which plays October–April at the MTS Centre in downtown Winnipeg, are a favourite.

How long to stay
Three days should be enough to hit both the downtown icons and outlying sights.

What's nearby
Lake Winnipeg, Whiteshell Provincial Park; Portage la Prairie.

When to go
Winnipeg winters are cold and windy, but the chilly months are home to some of the best events. The Festival du Voyageur in St. Boniface celebrates both the winter and the region's paddling pioneers with music and dance, snow sculptures and French-Canadian cuisine. Other highlights include the Jazz Festival in June and the Fringe Theatre Festival in July.

Canada's finest natural and human history collections. Continuous renovations and additions—including immersive, animated, hands-on exhibits such as Ancient Seas—give the museum a 21st-century feel, where technology blends entertainment with learning. Individual galleries are dedicated to Manitoba's history from prehistoric through modern times, as well as the province's distinct landscapes, including the Arctic, boreal forest, grasslands and urban areas. The Planetarium explores the outer reaches of the universe, while the recently reworked Science Gallery features new interactive encounters, such as "CSI" (solving murders with forensic techniques) and "Engineering for Speed" (build and test your own race car).

In royal company Canada's Royal Winnipeg Ballet is the longest continuous ballet company in North America.

Indoor shopping The Forks Market Courtyard blends a fresh food emporium with gourmet goodies and specialty art and craft stores.

Founded in 1939 and granted its royal title in 1953, the RWB has performed in nearly 600 cities worldwide and offers a wide range of local options from full-blown stage productions to recreational dance classes.

On the south side of Centennial Square, the Royal Manitoba Theatre Centre on Market Avenue was Canada's first regional theatre company and is still one of the most successful. MTC produces more than 250 plays per year and anchors a Winnipeg Theatre District that spans a dozen blocks around Old Market Square.

The Forks

Located on the southeast side of downtown, where the Assiniboine empties into the Red River, the Forks is a historic site, social rendezvous, marketplace and parkland area that draws both locals and visitors. Six thousand years of local history played out on these riverbanks, which functioned as a meeting place for Aboriginals, fur traders, settlers and soldiers. Parks Canada offers one-hour tours by rangers clad in historic garb, as well as GPS history hunts.

A number of historic structures have been adapted to modern uses. An old railway repair depot called the Boilers & Brakes Building (1889) is now the excellent Manitoba Children's Museum. Two old stables have been connected by a glass atrium and transformed into a mosaic of eateries and special shops called the Forks Market & Johnston Terminal.

More than 150 native plant species dominate the park's Prairie Garden, while the futuristic Esplanade Riel pedestrian bridge (designed by local French-Canadian architect Étienne Gaboury) leads to the city's French Quarter. Another ultramodern structure at the park's north end is the Canadian Museum for

The square's other big attraction is a modern arts complex, launched in 1968, that includes a large concert hall and theatre centre. The hall is the home base of the Manitoba Opera Company, the Winnipeg Symphony Orchestra and Royal Winnipeg Ballet, the country's premier ballet company.

Hudson's Bay Company

Headquartered in Winnipeg from 1911 to 1987, the Hudson's Bay Company (HBC) was founded in London in 1670. HBC was granted a royal charter to develop the fur trade in the North American territories seized from France during the Seven Years War. Over the next two centuries, the company expanded over central and western Canada. Trade was its raison d'être, but HBC was also charged with exploring the Arctic and western territories, searching for the Northwest Passage, making contact with Aboriginal groups, encouraging Western settlement and providing transportation in remote areas.

Human Rights (opening in 2012), detailing the legacy of global hatred and oppression. River tours embark from the Fork's historic port between May and October.

Old St. Boniface

The largest French-Canadian settlement outside of Quebec, old St. Boniface grew up on the east bank of the Red River opposite downtown Winnipeg. The neighbourhood developed around a French Catholic mission established in 1818. Nearly 200 years later, St. Boniface retains many French place names and cultural institutions.

Le Musée de Saint-Boniface is lodged in Winnipeg's oldest building, an 1844 convent that at one time was home to Grey Nuns. The museum exhibits explore the history and culture of Manitoba's French and Métis communities. The adjacent St. Boniface Cathedral comprises two distinct structures: the remains of the imposing Romanesque-style 1906 church, which was gutted by a fire, and the new cathedral rising right behind it.

Manitoba artists. Fort Gibraltar in riverside Whittier Park is a faithful reconstruction of an early 19th-century North West Company bastion and fur-trading post. Living history presentations take place throughout the warmer months.

Farther upstream Riel House in the Minnetonka neighbourhood celebrates the life and times of Métis leader Louis Riel, who led two uprisings against the Canadian government in favour of local rights. His Red River Rebellion of 1869–70 led to the establishment of Manitoba province. Riel was arrested and executed for high treason in 1885, but he remains a beloved figure among French Canadians.

Urban Outskirts

Every Canadian coin in circulation—billions each year—as well as the metallic currency of 70 other nations ranging from Cuba to Yemen, is created at the Royal Canadian Mint in southeastern Winnipeg, established in 1976. Marked by a modern glass pyramid designed by Étienne Gaboury, the facility includes a money boutique where freshly minted coins can be purchased. Guided tours are given year-round.

Practically a bedroom suburb these days, Selkirk is only 22 kilometres north of Winnepeg. Founded as the Red River Colony in 1813, it was one of the first European civilian settlements west of the Great Lakes. Among its relics are the old Hudson's Bay Company post called Lower Fort Garry and the Marine Museum of Manitoba, with its collection of Lake Winnipeg and Red River artifacts.

The city's contemporary French-Canadian community flocks to Le Maison des artistes visuels francophones in the old red-brick city hall on Provencher Boulevard. In addition to a modern art gallery and numerous special events, the centre's sculpture garden displays the works of French-speaking

St. Boniface's remains The façade of the 1906 church, ruined by fire in 1968, towers over the graveyard, where the remains of pioneer-politician Louis Riel are buried.

POLAR BEAR WATCHING

Each autumn, between 800 and 1,200 polar bears migrate from their summer habitat in the mixed boreal forest and tundra in northern Manitoba to their winter digs on the sea ice of Hudson Bay. Their migration route goes in and around Churchill, making the isolated Canadian town the best place for encounters with the big white bear.

Planning:
Churchill can be reached by rail or air from Winnipeg. Polar bears are viewed on day trips on special "tundra buggies," helicopter excursions or overnight stays at wilderness lodges. However, they also wander into town almost daily during the autumn migration.

Leaving Winnipeg

WHITESHELL

This eclectic park gets its name from the cowrie shells once used in this region for trading by the Ojibwa and other native peoples. Large and rambling Whiteshell Provincial Park snuggles up against the Manitoba-Ontario frontier, dotted with a variety of woodlands, wetlands and granite outcrops of the Canadian Shield. Both summer and winter the park presents myriad opportunities for outdoor activities.

Whiteshell is also of historical and cultural significance. People have dwelt in the region for at least 8,000 years, leaving behind numerous artifacts, including distinctive petroforms (rock alignments), throughout the park. The Winnipeg River, one of two main rivers that run through the park (the other being Whiteshell River), was an important fur-trading route in the late 18th and early 19th centuries. By the late 1800s, the Canadian Pacific Railway had pushed through the southern part of Whiteshell. The coal-and-water outpost at Rennie is now the park headquarters and the partially submerged railway tunnels of Cross Lake are one of the park's favourite canoe routes.

PLANNING

Whiteshell is 200 kilometres east of Winnipeg on the Trans-Canada Highway. Other parts of the park can be accessed on Route 44 and Route 307. From cottages to camping, the park offers many varied places to stay. Get far away from the crowds on the 60-kilometre Mantario Trail, a six-day hike.

GRAND BEACH

Stranded more than a thousand miles from the nearest beach resort, Manitobans began flocking to Lake Winnipeg in 1916 when the Canadian Pacific extended a railway line to the south shore and built a waterfront resort where passengers could linger during the long summer days. It came to be called Grand Beach and grew into the nucleus of a string of small lakeshore holiday resorts called the East Beaches. The eastern end of the strand is now a provincial park with pristine sandy beaches and rolling dunes; the western end is dominated by a vintage 1930s boardwalk with restaurants, shops and other amusements. Although water sports are the main attraction, berry picking, biking and birdwatching are also popular. In winter the lake provides a prime venue for ice fishing, skating and outdoor hockey.

PLANNING

Grand Beach is about 100 kilometres north of Winnipeg via Highway 59. Big-name music

Outdoor playground Whiteshell's numerous lakes and trails translate into myriad recreational choices no matter what the season or weather.

groups raise the roof at the annual Manitoba Summerfest in late July. Moose Madness in October honours the region's trademark mammal with costumed fun runs, scavenger hunts and wildlife encounters.

♣ ⛷ 🛶 ⛵ 🦆

THE PAS

They say the aurora borealis shines year-round in The Pas, and it's far enough north to make that a possibility. Set in the boreal forest beyond the northern end of Lake Winnipeg, this busy little town blends a frontier feel with neatly tended gardens and picture postcard churches. The Pas takes its name from Fort Paskoyac,

Summertime fun Sun, white sand and sealike conditions make Grand Beach Manitoba's most popular summer resort.

a French fur-trading post first established in the 1740s. Strange and bizarre artifacts collected from around the globe fill the in-town Sam Waller Museum in the old brick courthouse. Aseneskak Casino is located beyond the north bank of the Saskatchewan River in the Opaskwayak Cree community. The wilderness around The Pas offers plenty of scope for canoeing, mountain biking and hiking in summer, and various cold-weather sports in winter. With underwater visibility reaching 10 metres, nearby Clearwater Lake is thought to be one of the world's most translucent lakes.

PLANNING
A canoe race, Indian princess pageant, fishing derby and Cree dancing, music and games are part of the Opaskwayak Indian Days in August. The biggest event of the winter is the Northern Manitoba Trappers' Festival in February, with dog races, chainsaw competitions and a song-and-dance stage show at the historic Lido Theatre.

♣ 🏛 🛶 ⛵ 🦆

PISEW FALLS

The whisky-coloured Grass River tumbles 13 metres over a rocky escarpment at Pisew Falls Provincial Park. The name of the falls means "lynx" in the Cree language, and it was called thus because the First Nation people thought the sound of the falls was like a growling wildcat. Rapids just below the falls empty into Brostrom Lake. A wilderness hiking trail and canoe passage leads upstream along the path of an 18th-century fur-trading route to Phillips

Loud display Making up with sound and fury what it lacks in height, Pisew Falls plunges through a gorge in northern Manitoba.

Lake Winnipeg

Winnipeg means "murky waters" in the language of the ancient Cree, but that hardly describes Manitoba's aquatic icon. Earth's tenth largest freshwater lake often takes a backseat to the more fabled Great Lakes, but it boasts just as many treasures. Created by glacial action during the last ice age, the lake's numerous feeders drain a huge portion of central North America before emptying into the Hudson Bay via the Nelson River. Many of its white-sand beaches seem scooped from the Caribbean, while its limestone cliffs resemble the rugged shores of the Maritimes. Commercial fishing (for whitefish, walleye and sauger) is still an important activity for lakeshore communities, many of them comprising Métis and First Nation residents.

Lake and 14-metre-high Kwasitchewan Falls, the highest in Manitoba. Otters, black bears and wolves are among the wildlife that dwell in the area.

PLANNING
The turnoff to Pisew Falls is 74 kilometres south of Thompson on Highway 6. Six primitive campsites are available upstream from Pisew. Otherwise, the closest accommodation is in Thompson.

♣ 🦆 ⛵ 🦆

A Dozen Great Heritage Sites in the Prairies

Mennonite Heritage Village

Hoping to attract more settlers to the Canadian prairies, the government recruited Russian Mennonite immigrants in the 1870s and awarded them free land in Manitoba. By 1878 there were around 3,000 Mennonites in the province, living in eight townships in what was called the East Reserve area. They introduced a typical European settlement pattern of villages surrounded by fields.

The Mennonite Heritage Village in Steinbach tells the story of these pioneers through architecture, artifacts and exhibits. At the heart of the collection are two dozen historical structures gathered from around the East Reserve, including sod and log dwellings, churches, a blacksmith shop, a school and a printer's shop. Among the more distinctive buildings are the 1892 Chortitz housebarn and the reconstructed Mennonite windmill—believed to be the only working mill in Canada.

The village is still a living Mennonite community. Vesper services are held in the Worship House on the first Sunday of every month. Wagon rides and equestrian demonstrations are part of the summer program.

Other Great Heritage Sites

Canadian Fossil Discovery Centre, Manitoba. The region's prehistoric heritage is the focus of this unique new natural history museum in Morden.

Inglis Grain Elevators, Manitoba. A row of five 1920s grain elevators are among the last of their kind in Canada, architectural symbols of the prairie region's formative years.

Lower Fort Garry, Manitoba. The oldest stone, trading fort in North America and the largest group of original 19th-century fur-trade buildings in Canada was created by the Hudson's Bay Company in 1830.

Manitoba Antique Automobile Museum, Manitoba. A 1908 Reo and 1909 Hupmobile are among the hundred vehicles in this eclectic Elkhorn collection, which also includes vintage weapons, farm equipment and First Nation artifacts.

York Factory, Manitoba. This remote outpost on the shore of Hudson Bay served as an HBC trading post for 273 years (1684–1957) and the main gateway to European immigration to Western Canada for much of the 19th century.

Batoche, Saskatchewan. Métis insurgent leader Louis Riel chose Batoche as the capital of his breakaway government during the Northwest Rebellion and fought government forces there on May 9–12, 1885.

Cannington Manor, Saskatchewan. Fox hunts, cricket matches and poetry readings were part of daily life at this Victorian-era utopian community created by upper-class British immigrants.

Doukhobor Heritage Village, Saskatchewan. This village honours the thousands of Doukhobor Christians who immigrated from Russia to the Canadian prairies in the 1890s.

Fort Battleford, Saskatchewan. Five original buildings remain at a bastion that once served the North West Mounted Police between 1876 and 1924.

Fort Walsh, Saskatchewan. Established in 1875, this Cypress Hills landmark was once the largest and most important North West Mounted Police outpost on the western frontier.

Motherwell Homestead, Saskatchewan. Built in the 1880s, Lanarck Place and the surrounding farmland honour the memory of pioneer agronomist and politician W.R. Motherwell.

The village quilters demonstrate and preserve that vital Mennonite art form. And typical Mennonite dishes—komst borscht, foarma worscht, kielkje and rhubarb plautz—are served in the village restaurant.

Planning: Steinbach is 65 kilometres southeast of Winnipeg via the Trans-Canada Highway and provincial route 12. Steinbach offers several motels for those who want to stay overnight. Nearby Mennonite-founded villages include Grunthal, Rosengard, Blumenort and Kleefeld.

Western Manitoba

PORTAGE LA PRAIRIE

Situated on plains between Lake Manitoba and the Assiniboine River, explorer and fur trader Pierre Gaultier de Varennes decided to build a fort and trading post here in 1738 in what was then the westernmost extent of European influence on the Great Plains. The town grew up in the 1850s around Crescent Lake—an oxbow that was once part of the Assiniboine River—when it was realized that the region's fertile soil was ideal for farming. Today, Crescent Lake forms the nucleus of local recreation, social life and tourism. In addition to myriad migratory birds, Island Park in the middle of the lake boasts a golf course, twin ice arenas, indoor swimming pools and a water park called Splash Island.

Fort la Reine Museum on the town's eastern edge spins the history of the Canadian prairies from ancient times to the early 20th century, including two dozen historic structures from elsewhere in the province.

PLANNING

Visit in winter for cold-weather sports (cross-country skiing, snowshoeing, skating), and for Island of Lights, a Christmas lights extravaganza from November to January.

NEEPAWA

With more than 2,000 varieties of lily grown in the area, Neepawa calls itself the "Lily Capital of the World." Even without its flowers, the town is one of Manitoba's most attractive, flush with Victorian-era buildings, leafy parks and scenic waterways. The name means "land of plenty" in the language of the Cree people, who populated this region before European settlement. Neepawa was also the birthplace and last resting place of celebrated Canadian writer Margaret Laurence (1926–87), whose home is now a museum and national historic site. Her fictional Manawaka of novels, such as *The Stone Angel* and *A Jest of God,* are based on mid-20th-century Neepawa. The Beautiful Plains Museum, housed in the old clapboard CNR train station, covers a range of local history, from pioneer days through to locals who fought in both world wars.

Canada's breadbasket With two main train lines and a booming agriculture, Portage La Prairie has been transformed from a one-horse frontier town into the little dynamo of western Manitoba.

Flower power Neepawa's tourism and economy relies on its floral production—not only do blooms colour the region, but bulbs are exported around the world.

PLANNING
The Neepawa Lily Festival in late July showcases the best of local blossoms, as well as live entertainment, food stalls, quilt shows, pioneer dances and cabarets.
🏛 ⚘

BRANDON
Straddling the Assiniboine River, Brandon is the province's second largest city as well as a major transportation and agricultural hub. The Gothic revival-style St. Matthew's Cathedral (1913) anchors a downtown area known for gorgeous brick buildings. Architect W.A. Elliott created a number of other Brandon landmarks, including the flamboyant Central Fire Station (1911). Among Brandon's many museums are the Art Gallery of Western Manitoba and two fine military collections: the Commonwealth Air Training Plan Museum and its historic aircraft at Brandon Airport, and the Royal Canadian Artillery Museum at CFB Shilo. The Assiniboine Riverbank Trail System provides 17 kilometres of walking, biking and equestrian paths linking the downtown area to parks, sporting venues and forested areas.

PLANNING
Various music events include the Brandon Folk Festival in July (which often draws world-renowned artists), the Brandon Jazz Festival in March and the Brandon University School of Music Pro Series from September to April.
🌲 🏛 🖼

SPRUCE WOODS
Located 85 kilometres east of Brandon, Spruce Woods Provincial Park protects a large area of spruce woodland and mixed grass prairie along the Assiniboine River. The park's most unique feature is a desertlike area called the Spirit Sands, the relic of a long-ago glacial delta that includes rolling dunes and pincushion cactus. By summer the park is a paradise for hikers, horseback riders, mountain bikers and paddlers. By winter the extensive trail system is the realm of cross-country skiers and snowmobilers.

PLANNING
The only drive-in campground is Kiche Manitou, but there are five backcountry campsites. Motel-style accommodation is available in Carberry and Glenboro.
🌲 🐦 ⛷

RIDING MOUNTAIN
An island of woodland in the middle of a grassy sea, Riding Mountain National Park straddles the Manitoba Escarpment. It has just enough elevation to transform the landscape from prairie into a boreal forest with wetlands and numerous lakes. Wildlife in the region is abundant: there are moose, elk, bison, wolf, beaver and one of the world's largest black bear populations. Opened in 1933, many of the visitor facilities date from that time, built as part of Canada's great depression relief program. Noted British-Canadian conservationist Grey Owl (a.k.a. Archibald Belaney), his Native American wife Anahareo and their two pet beavers lived at Riding Mountain briefly during the early 1930s and their cabin is now a park landmark. The park was also home to a Second World War POW camp that housed German prisoners.

PLANNING
Summer events include a square-dancing jamboree, prison camp tour in a horse-drawn wagon, golf and tennis tournaments, and a chamber music festival.
🌲 🏛 🐦 ⛷ 🏄 🐟

Mountain denizen Black bear are among the wildlife living on Riding Mountain, a heavily forested national park in the middle of the Manitoba prairie.

Regina Sights and Sounds

From an uninspiring past, Saskatchewan's capital of Regina has emerged as the attractive city it is today with manicured lawns and mild-mannered ways.

Its original name was Wascana, the Cree term for "pile of bones," a reference to the countless buffalo remains left behind by First Nation and Métis hunters. The town was founded in 1882 as a railway whistle stop and capital of the Northwest Territories. Arriving on the first train, Princess Louise (daughter of Queen Victoria and wife of Canada's Governor General) optimistically christened the town "Regina" after her mother. At the time Regina was better known for mud, dust and boredom. The vibe didn't change until 1905, when Regina

became capital of the new Saskatchewan province. Filled with determination, the citizenry planted trees, morphed their muddy waterway into an attractive park and brought culture to the prairies. A century later, Regina is the province's commercial, political and cultural core, a genteel city with a superb quality of life and booming economy.

Wascana Centre

Regina's heart is a mosaic of green and blue called Wascana Centre. The green space, Canada's fourth largest urban park, began to take shape in the late 1800s, when Wascana Creek was damned to create a serpentine lake through the city. The park's overall design wasn't formalized until 1962, when

Boat tour Saskatchewan's Legislative Building rises above tranquil Wascana Lake, the centrepiece of Regina's largest park.

Oasis in the city For more than a hundred years, Victoria Park has offered a tranquil green escape among the surrounding office blocks of downtown Regina.

the city hired Japanese-American architect Minoru Yamasaki to draw up a master plan in concert with his design for the new Regina campus of the University of Saskatchewan.

The imposing beaux art-style Saskatchewan Legislative Building (1912), constructed with 34 different types of marble from all around the globe, looms above the lake's western end. Galleries inside the building showcase Canadian art, including many pieces by First Nation artists. Among the landmarks in the surroundings gardens are a fountain that once graced London's Trafalgar Square.

Don't Miss

Mackenzie Art Gallery
The province's premier art venue showcases both western Canadian art in all its shapes and forms and the work of 19th- and 20th-centuries European artists such as Degas, Gainsborough, Munch and Picasso.

Regina Plains Museum
This city museum presents rotating exhibits on various aspects of the urban past, as well as two stunning permanent works: the "Community Mural" by Sherry Farrell Racette and "The Glass Wheatfield" by Jacqueline Berting, which comprises 14,000 individually crafted glass wheat stalks.

Qu'Appelle Valley
Located a short drive northeast of Regina, the lush lowlands along the Qu'Appelle River are filled with tranquil lakes and picture postcard farms. In addition to many native plant and animal species, the valley is also home to Cree, Saulteaux and Dakota and other First Nations people.

On the other side of Albert Street Bridge is the Royal Saskatchewan Museum, with one of the nation's finest natural history collections. Its mascot is "Megamunch," a full-scale robotic *Tyrannosaurus rex*. The Life Science Gallery details the province's various natural regions, while the First Nation Gallery examines the culture and lifestyles of the region's native peoples. Farther east along the lakeshore is the Saskatchewan Science Centre, with a modern, hands-on museum designed to get kids interested in science.

Along Dewdney Avenue
The Royal Canadian Mounted Police (RCMP) Heritage Center on Dewdney Avenue in south Regina tells how the Mounties were

City Insider

Words to the wise
Regina Transit offers day/weekend family passes good for unlimited rides on municipal buses.

Locals love it
The Saskatchewan Roughriders are the town's professional football team, and play June to November at Mosaic Stadium. Their supporters are ranked as the rowdiest sports fans in Canada.

How long to stay
Two days (three nights) is just about right for exploring the major highlights of Regina.

What's nearby
Moose Jaw; Buffalo Point Provincial Park; Regina Beach at Last; Mountain Lake; Big Muddy Badlands.

When to go
At the end of November, Wascana Centre starts to morph into a winter wonderland of snow-covered trees and frozen water. The Regina Ski Club maintains cross-country trails around the park and the Prairie Pond Hockey Challenge takes place on the lake.

transformed into one of the world's most respected law-enforcement agents. Right behind the museum is the RCMP Academy (Depot Division). Visitors can watch the Sunset-Retreat Ceremony, which includes a march past and military music and drills, and flag-lowering ceremony performed by cadets.

Farther east along Dewdney Avenue is the Government House Museum, an Italianate-style mansion that served as the home of lieutenant-governors of the Northwest Territories and Saskatchewan from 1891 to 1945. Just around the corner is the sprawling Evraz Place (Regina Exhibition Park), home to major regional events such as Buffalo Days (now called the Queen City Ex) and the Western Canada Farm Progress Show.

Central and Eastern Saskatchewan

SASKATOON

Saskatchewan's largest city takes its name from the Cree word for a sweet dark berry found in the region. Founded in 1883 by the Temperance Colonization Society, the city started life as a "dry" town among rough and tumble prairies. Nowadays, the population is a dynamic mix of German, Ukrainian and Anglo–Irish communities, plus large Métis and First Nation components. Farming and mining (in particular, potash and uranium) fuel the local economy, with biotech rising fast. Despite modern skyscrapers, the chateau-style Delta Bessborough Hotel (1935) still dominates the city's South Saskatchewan River waterfront. Contemporary and historical art, much

of it with a regional bent, are the forte of the Mendel Art Gallery. The adjacent City Conservatory provides a leafy winter hangout and a Zen garden for those who need to chill out at any time of year. Two of Saskatoon's more prominent ethnic groups are the focus of the Ukrainian Museum of Canada and the Wanuskewin Heritage Park with its First Nation archaeological sites.

PLANNING

There is a diverse range of summer events, from Shakespeare on the Saskatchewan riverside to an adrenalin-packed WakeRide, with competition wakeboarding, skateboarding and motocross.

MANITOU BEACH

Like the Dead Sea of the Middle East and Karlovy Vary in the Czech Republic, the waters of Manitou Lake in central Saskatchewan are suffused with salts and minerals purported to have therapeutic qualities. "Lake of the Healing Waters" is what the Cree called it, and thousands flock to the small lakeshore resort each year to soak or float in water so dense that it's nearly impossible to sink. Visitors can take a dip in the lake or relax indoors at the Manitou Springs Spa, where the mineralized water is heated to three different temperatures. Located next to the spa is Danceland, which was built in 1928 and is renown for its horsehair dance floor.

PLANNING

Most facilities are located in the village of Manitou Beach on the lake's south shore.

Waterfront property Saskatoon's historic Broadway Bridge spans across the South Saskatchewan River. The Delta Bessborough Hotel is to the right.

Lakeside attraction As well as being a bird sanctuary, Last Mountain Lake is enjoyed by outdoor enthusiasts.

LAST MOUNTAIN LAKE

North America's oldest bird sanctuary, Last Mountain Lake was established in 1887. The reserve is home to nine of the nation's 36 endangered avian species, including the peregrine falcon, whooping crane, burrowing owl and Caspian tern. At the peak of the autumn migratory season as many as half a million geese, several hundred thousand duck and 45,000 sandhill crane have been counted in the wetlands at the lake's north end. Located beneath North America's central flyway, the sanctuary is one of a network of 94 scattered across Canada and has been designated a wetlands of international importance. Birdwatchers also flock to the nearby Quill Lakes International Bird Area, where more than 300 species (and 300,000 birds per day) have been counted. Visitors can explore the area by foot on grassland and wetland trails.

PLANNING

The information kiosk is 24 kilometres northeast of Imperial, Saskatchewan.

MOOSE MOUNTAIN

A mosaic of woods and water, Moose Mountain Provincial Park blends hundreds of lakes with thick birch, maple and aspen forest in a rolling highlands area that rises above the plains of southeastern Saskatchewan. Kenosee Lake, the largest of these water bodies, is the park hub and where the bulk of water activities (swimming, boating, fishing) unfold. A huge network of trails—good for hiking and biking in summer, cross-country skiing, snowmobiling or snowshoeing in winter—leads into the backcountry. Moose Mountain also boasts a golf course, tennis courts and other sports facilities. The resort village of Kenosee Lake perches on the north shore of the eponymous lake.

PLANNING

Cabins and camping are available at Kenosee Lake. The park visitor centre is in the same area, inside a historic stone chalet overlooking the lake.

YORKTON

Established in 1882 by settlers from York City, Ontario, this small but busy town lies astride the Trans-Canada Highway in a region dotted with farms and small glacial lakes. The local branch of the Saskatchewan Western Development Museum highlights the role of immigrants in the settlement of the prairies through exhibits that reflect the cultures and lifestyles of émigré Ukrainians, Germans, Scandinavians, Russian Doukhobors and others. The only public art museum within a 150-kilometre radius, the Godfrey Dean Art Gallery exhibits artists who address issues affecting the region. The Yorkton Film Festival is an internationally renowned cinema showcase with screenings by some of Canada's best-known filmmakers.

PLANNING

The Yorkton Film Festival is a four-day event that takes the stage each May.

Trail well travelled Visit Moose Mountain in autumn as the leaves change colour for the best experience.

CASTLE BUTTE

Formed during the last ice age, Castle Butte
towers 70 metres above the Big Muddy Badlands
of southeast Saskatchewan. The sandstone mount
was once a landmark in an otherwise featureless
landscape for the First Nation peoples, notorious
outlaws and mounted police who visited this region.
Nowadays, it's a popular hike and photo
opportunity, best at dusk and dawn,
when the butte often glows
red or orange.

Planning:
Castle Butte is about a 40-minute drive
southwest of Bengough, Saskatchewan. Drive
Highway 34 south for about 18 kilometres, turn
right onto an unmarked road and head west for
about 7 kilometres until the butte appears.

MOOSE JAW

"Little Chicago of the Prairies" earned its notorious nom-de-plume during American Prohibition, when local bootleggers teamed up with Al Capone and other gangsters to smuggle booze below the border. The city's past can be explored in the Tunnels of Moose Jaw, a system of basements and connecting tunnels beneath downtown. Downtown's other claim to fame is the Murals of Moose Jaw, a series of 45 scenes that depict the city's pioneer past and early history. The Western Development Museum on the north side delves into the history of prairie transport from the canoes and travois of the First Nation peoples to the local RCAF Snowbirds aerial acrobatic squadron.

PLANNING

In July the Saskatchewan Festival of Words celebrates the written word in all its forms (in any language). In August the Connect Festival

Southern Saskatchewan

GRASSLANDS

Created in 1981, Grasslands National Park protects a pristine stretch of mixed-grass prairie in southern Saskatchewan along the border with Montana. More than 70 grass species can be found within the park's boundaries, complemented by more than 50 varieties of wildflower, a floral display that is especially vibrant in spring. Wildlife is also bountiful, including many animals that rare elsewhere in Canada such as the pronghorn antelope, prairie rattlesnake, black-footed ferret and burrowing owl. Grasslands also has an interesting human history. Scattered across the park are more than 12,000 ancient teepee rings, and it was here that Sitting Bull and his Sioux warriors found refuge after the Battle of the Little Bighorn in 1876. The

Killdeer Badlands of the park's East Block is where Sir George Mercer Dawson discovered western Canada's first dinosaur remains and the area remains one of the world's richest fossil beds. With so little settlement around the park, Grasslands is has been designated the nation's darkest Dark Sky Preserve, and is an ideal place to observe the night sky.

PLANNING

The park's Visitor Reception Centre is near Val Marie, about 365 kilometres from Regina. The West Block is easily explored by car, but the remote East Block is nearly inaccessible. Only primitive camping is allowed in the park; accommodation is available in Val Marie and other local nearby communities.
🌲 ⛺ 🐦

Notorious connections Moose Jaw's nefarious past includes encounters with Al Capone and other gangland figures.

brings a mix of electronic and tribal music to a location 60 kilometres west of Moose Jaw on the Trans-Canada Highway.
👪 🏛 🖼

BIG MUDDY

Formed by glacial melt during the last ice age and weathered significantly since, the Big Muddy Badlands is a series of sandstone and clay badlands in a valley of the same name that straddles the international border between Saskatchewan and Montana. The most significant formation is 70-metre Castle Butte, which is easily climbed for a view of the badlands. The remote, largely uninhabited region was a hideout for Canadian and American outlaws around the turn of the 20th century and the northernmost point on an "Outlaw Trail" that stretched all the way to Mexico. Local history is suffused with myth and legend, but it's said that Butch Cassidy, Dutch Henry and Sam Kelly were among those who visited the badlands. The town museum in Willow Bunch describes the region's heritage, including the personal effects of Edouard Beaupré (1881–1904), the 2.5-metre-tall "Willow Bunch Giant." The region's other attraction is the St. Victor Petroglyphs, a collection of animal and bird figures, abstract forms and human foot and handprints rendered on a sandstone cliff. Researchers have yet to determine who created the figures or why.

PLANNING
The northern end of the Big Muddy Badlands is about 200 kilometres southwest of Regina via provincial highways 6 and 13. The town of Coronach offers human and natural history tours of the area July to early September.
🌲 🏛 🪑

EASTEND

Tucked in the southwest of Saskatchewan, the village of Eastend is renowned for its dinosaurs. Most famous of these is

The Mounties

Canada's famed Mounties started life as the North West Mounted Police, a paramilitary law-enforcement group formed in 1873 by the Canadian Parliament at the behest of first prime minister Sir John A. Macdonald. Based on the Royal Irish Constabulary, the mounted force was charged with the task of bringing law and order, making peace with the native peoples and stamping Canadian authority on the remote North West Territories (today's Saskatchewan and Alberta). From the very start, the Mounties wore the scarlet-coloured jacket that would become their symbol. The unit's trademark Stetson hat wasn't added until the 1890s. One of their first outposts was Fort Walsh (1875) in southern Saskatchewan, the NWMP headquarters for a number of years. The Mounties were instrumental in ending the Northwest Rebellion of 1885 and were dispatched to the Yukon during the Klondike Gold Rush. They also saw action overseas, in the Boer War and First World War. Their frontier days long gone, the name was changed to Royal Canadian Mounted Police in 1920.

"Scotty," the *Tyrannosaurus rex*, residing at the T. rex Discovery Centre. Operated by the Royal Saskatchewan Museum, the ultramodern facility offers exhibits, films, talks and workshops on various aspects of paleontology and dinosaurs. Eastend's other landmark is the Wallace Stegner House, where the celebrated Western author lived between the ages of 7 and 12.

PLANNING
Don't miss Dino Days, an annual mélange of parades, rodeos and other events in July.
👪 🏛 🪑

Frightful delight "Scotty" the dinosaur, discovered in the nearby Frenchman Formation in 1994, is the superstar of Eastend's museum.

Northern Saskatchewan

Special occasion Prince Albert and environs host a number of First Nation and Métis festivals and other events each year.

PRINCE ALBERT

Saskatchewan's "Gateway to the North" lies in the transition zone between the prairies and the boreal forest. The province's third largest city is a transport and agricultural hub, as well as a focal point of Métis culture. The Prince Albert Historical Museum, located in the old Central Fire Hall (1912), details the city's evolution from 18th-century fur-trading post into a frontier metropolis that was renamed for Queen Victoria's husband in 1904. Two other small, somewhat quirky collections are housed in the city's visitor centre on Highway 2: the Rotary Museum of Police and Corrections, and the Evolution of Education Museum.

PLANNING

Prince Albert and and the surrounding area host a number of First Nation cultural events such as the Métis Fall Festival in September, with its traditional fiddling, jigging and square dancing, as well as Métis foods and arts and crafts.

LAC LA RONGE

Centred around a large lake of the same name, Lac La Ronge Provincial Park unfolds as a paradise of islands, water and thick boreal forest far removed from both the prairies and the bustle of urban Saskatchewan. Visitors explore the area by canoe, sailboat and houseboat, although hiking and biking trails are also available. The year-round reserve turns its attention to cross-country skiing, snowshoeing and lake fishing come winter. The old Stanley Mission sits on the banks of the Churchill River on the park's northern fringe, crowned by the Gothic-revival style Holy Trinity Anglican Church (1854), the oldest building in Saskatchewan.

PLANNING

Lac La Ronge is located about 2½ hours north of Prince Albert via Highway 2. Roads run into the heart of the park all the way to Stanley Mission, but most of the area is only accessible by boat or foot.

GREY OWL TRAIL

Located in Prince Albert National Park, the 20-kilometre wilderness route honours pioneer environmentalist Grey Owl (see right), who resided in the park for much of the 1930s. Starting from the Kingsmere River parking lot, the trail takes about six hours to walk, much of it along the eastern shore of Kingsmere Lake. Visitors can also negotiate much of the route via canoe or kayak. Historic Beaver Lodge perches on the shore of the smaller Ajawaan Lake. Grey Owl, his wife and their daughter, Shirley Dawn, are buried in a nearby cemetery. Wildlife in the park is profuse, including a herd of free-roaming bison and a large colony of white pelicans (up to 15,000 birds) at Lavallée Lake.

PLANNING

The nearest campsite is 3 kilometres from the lodge at the north end of Kingsmere

Floating home With more than half the park covered by water, houseboats are a popular means of exploring Lac La Ronge.

Lake. There are half a dozen other campsites around the lakeshore. Visitors staying overnight must obtain a backcountry-use permit beforehand.

🌲 🏛 🚻 🦅 🛶

ATHABASCA

One of Canada's strangest landscapes, the desertlike wilderness of Athabasca Sand Dunes stretches for about 100 kilometres along the south shore of Lake Athabasca. This is the nation's largest accumulation of sand, with far more granules than anywhere on the Atlantic or Pacific coasts. It's also one of the planet's most northerly dune fields, totally out of place in the boreal backwoods. Strange plants flourish in the unique and fragile sandy wasteland, with endemic species such as Mackenzie hairgrass and fluccose tansy found nowhere else on Earth, an evolutionary puzzle even to scientists. Dene First Nation myth holds that the dunes were created by a giant beaver kicking up sand; the scientific explanation is that the strange landforms are the result of glacial retreat after the last ice age.

PLANNING

With no roads into the area, the only way to reach the Athabasca Dunes is to book a boat or float plane. There are six primitive campsites within the provincial park that protects the site.

🌲 🚻 🛶

Grey Owl's Legacy

Born in England, Archibald Belaney emmigrated to Canada in 1906, immersed himself in Aboriginal culture and eventually took the name Grey Owl. After two decades as a fur trapper and hunting guide in northern Ontario, he married a Mohawk woman named Anahareo and moved to the prairie provinces, where his vision of nature transformed from destruction to ardent preservation. His eloquent writings helped spark the Canadian environmental movement in much the same way as John Muir in the United States, leading to his appointment in the early 1930s as the first naturalist of Parks Canada. After living for a brief time at Riding Mountain National Park in Manitoba, Grey Owl, Anahareo and their pet beavers (Rawhide and Jelly Roll) moved to Prince Albert National Park in Saskatchewan. During his time at the park's Beaver Lodge, he penned three bestselling books: *Pilgrims of the Wild* (1934), *Sajo and the Beaver People* (1935) and *Empty Cabin* (1936). Grey Owl died of pneumonia at the lakeside retreat in 1938.

On a wing and a ski The only reasonable way to reach the Athabasca Sands is by float plane across the wilds of northern Saskatchewan.

the WEST

Southern Alberta

Giant tepee Under the Saamis tepee in Medicine Hat is the site of an ancient buffalo camp. Archaeologists believe there are thousands of artifacts buried here.

MEDICINE HAT

The Trans-Canada Highway takes travellers into the heart of "The Hat," the first major Alberta town west of Saskatchewan. The city sits in the valley of the South Saskatchewan River and bills itself as Canada's "sunniest city," with a record number of sunny days each year. Its Blackfoot name is "Saamis," meaning "Medicine Man's Hat," although differing legends relate its origins. The Saamis Tepee, created for the 1988 Calgary Olympics and moved three years later to Medicine Hat, is 65.5 metres high and features ten storyboards about the local Aboriginal culture.

Early industries built up around the area's rich clay and natural gas deposits. The large Historic Clay District houses the former Medalta Potteries Factory, now a museum, as well as a contemporary gallery, workshops, and artists-in-residence. South of the city, Cypress Hills Interprovincial Park traverses the border of Saskatchewan and Alberta. The high plateaus are home to many different birds and animals and offer camping and fishing facilities at Reesor Lake and Elkwater.

PLANNING

Catch the Medicine Hat Exhibition and Stampede in the summer for western rodeo shows and entertainment.

👫 🏛 🎨 🐦 🐟

HEAD-SMASHED-IN

This UNESCO World Heritage Site is one of North America's oldest and best-preserved buffalo jumps, sites at which Plains people killed large numbers of buffalo, herding them over the cliffs, and using the flat land below for butchering. Archaeologists confirmed that Head-Smashed-In Buffalo Jump was such a site by studying the gathering basin, where buffalo grazed, and the stone cairns leading to the driving lanes through which hunters herded the animals. In addition, bones, arrowheads and other evidence found at the bottom of the cliff points to the site's use more than 5,700 years ago. After the arrival of the Europeans and the railway in the 1800s, grazing lands were depleted and bison were hunted for sport. As a result here and in other places in North America, the bison almost disappeared altogether. Head-Smashed-In's interpretive centre provides details of the buffalo jump and chronicles the history of the Blackfoot people, before and after European arrival.

PLANNING

Located 18 kilometres northwest of Fort Macleod, special events such as powwows run year-round. Check before going; inclement weather may cause temporary closures.

👫 🏛

Ancient hunt Head-Smashed-In holds the remains of many buffalo skeletons. Hunters butchered the meat on the land below the cliffs.

Frank Landslide

At 4:10 a.m. on April 29, 1903, in just 90 seconds, 30 million cubic metres of limestone slid from the top of Turtle Mountain and crashed on Frank, the town below. Much of the town lay beyond the crash site, but about 70 people died in the landslide. An interpretive centre relays information about "Frank Slide," as well as the natural and cultural history of the area. Frank and other towns in the valley of the continental divide of Crowsnest Pass were mining communities, and the industry likely contributed to the mountain's instability. Crowsnest Pass is a stunning geological feature of the area.

LETHBRIDGE

The Blackfoot called the area *sik-okotoks*, or "Place of Black Rocks," because of the coal, and this industry drove the economy from the 1870s. Oil, natural gas and agriculture took over, and Lethbridge became an important distribution centre in the early 20th century. Visit the Galt Museum and Archives to discover Southwestern Alberta's past. One of the city's memorable sights is the Canadian Pacific Railway bridge, a steel trestle bridge built in 1909. Measuring 1.6 kilometres from end to end, the bridge is still the longest of its type in the world. Another stop is Fort Whoop-Up. American traders established the fort in 1869 as Fort Hamilton, but it gained its nickname from its reputation as an outpost for illegal whisky and arms trading. The Mounties stopped the trading and fire later destroyed the fort, but a stone and plaque mark the site. A reconstructed fort, built nearby in Indian Battle Park, sits on the site of the last inter-tribal battle between the Cree and the Blackfoot. The Nikka Yuko Japanese Garden, which blends the beauty of the rugged landscape with the elegance of Japanese design, was established in 1967 in honour of the town's Japanese citizens.

PLANNING

Allow a day to see Lethbridge but more to see nearby attractions, including Alberta's Birds of Prey Centre in Coaldale, Fort Macleod and Waterton-Glacier International Peace Park.
👫 🏛

Spiritual messages Rock art is difficult to date, but specific images, such as horses, suggest later carvings. Aboriginal elders still visit Writing-on-Stone to seek direction in these images from the spirit world.

WRITING-ON-STONE

The culturally significant Writing-on-Stone Provincial Park has the largest collection of petroglyphs and pictographs in North America. Called *Áísínai'pi* by the Blackfoot, the area is a spiritual place to Aboriginal people for whom the cliffs and hoodoos hold sacred powers. There is archaeological evidence of rock art in the park's sandstone cliffs dating back 3,000 years. At the end of the 1800s, the North West Mounted Police used the area as a policing post to stop whisky smuggling across the American–Canadian border, but border posts were closed by 1918. Visitors can tour a reconstructed police post. The area later became a heritage parkland. The park is located in a valley surrounding the Milk River, and the vast, grassy landscape is replete with sandstone hoodoos, 3–10 metres high. The park's trails offer access to the ancient art with an Aboriginal guide and wildlife watching. As hikers walk the main 2.5-kilometre trail, they may spot pronghorn, deer, salamanders or gophers, or one of many bird species known to nest in the area.

PLANNING

The park has day-use facilities and campsites open year round; reservations are available.
🌲 ⛺ 🏛 🐦

The Western Spirit of Calgary

Soaring buildings and a young, cosmopolitan population may belie Calgary's "Cow Town" past, but its Wild West hospitality is still there in spades.

First populated by Plains tribes, the railway brought ranchers to Calgary, and the town's western image was born. The ranchers were seduced by government grants and stretches of land ideal for cattle grazing. Even today, Calgary is the centre of the cattle industry in Canada. However, rich oil deposits nearby transformed the city from a ranching community into an oil boom town. This prosperity lasted from the 1940s until the early 1980s. In the years since Calgary has rebounded as a multi-faceted city with premiere arts and science centres, international businesses and nature parks.

Frontier Town

Calgary's downtown core is dense with glass and steel architecture, but vestiges of the city's history remain. After a fire in 1886 destroyed many of Calgary's wooden structures, builders began using local, Paskapoo sandstone to construct buildings. The Grain Exchange Building, the old City Hall and the Fairmont Palliser Hotel are among the prominent sandstone buildings still being used today in "Sandstone City."

Calgary's frontier spirit comes to life at Heritage Park Historical Village, a 51-hectare park dedicated to the western experience. As well as a replica town, wagon rides and a themed midway, there's a steam train and paddlewheeler. For more Wild West fun, the Glenbow Museum tells the story of Alberta, including an exhibit on the Blackfoot. The Wild West Event Centre is the place to see a rodeo or ride a mechanical bull.

City Sights

To see the streets stretch out of Calgary, east to the prairies and west to the mountains, take a ride to the top of the Calgary Tower. Opened in 1968, Calgary's iconic structure looms 191 metres above the city. On a clear day many of Calgary's attractions such as Fort Calgary and Calgary Zoo are visible. The zoo, one of the finest in Canada, takes over half of St. George's Island in the heart of the city.

Saddledome Now a Calgary landmark, the arena hosted events during the 1988 Olympics. Today, it is home to the city's hockey and football teams.

Greatest Outdoor Show on Earth

Not only is the Calgary Stampede one of the world's largest rodeo shows, it also hosts one of the country's largest music festivals, a chuckwagon derby and a mobile midway. A group of wealthy ranchers decided to hold the city's first rodeo in 1912. Since then, the ten-day event takes over the city every July, and for many, the Stampede is the essence of the Calgary experience.

Canada Olympic Park
Visit the park where history happened and use the top-notch sports facilities. In the winter go skiing or take a luge ride. In warmer months take a mountain bike for a spin. Under 16s can climb the Spiderweb or bounce on the Eurobungy.

Bow Habitat Station
Learn all about the area's wildlife and conservation at this eco-park just east of Calgary Zoo, on the Bow River. Watch trout at the Sam Livingston Fish Hatchery begin their aquatic journey and learn about marsh and stream life at the Pearce Estate Park Interpretive Wetland.

Calaway Park
If you love rides, this amusement park just west of Calgary is a treat for the entire family. An RV park and campsites ensure the fun lasts for more than a day.

Telus Spark Science Centre is a short drive north of the zoo. Younger scientists will love the Creative Kids Museum.

Olympian and Outdoor Pursuits
In 1988 Calgary became the first Canadian city to host the winter Olympics. Today, Canada Olympic Park (COP) is still used by world-class athletes, but the facilities are open to the general public for winter and summer sports. Activities at the venue include skiing and snowboarding, zip lining and mountain biking. An experience for thrill-seekers is the bobsleigh ride in winter or summer, an unforgettable adventure piloted by a professional driver. While visiting the Olympic Park, stop by Canada's Sports

City Insider

Words to the wise
The C Train, part of Calgary's public transit system, is free in the downtown core, but fees apply if you leave the area.

Locals love it
The world's best speed skaters train at the University of Calgary's Olympic Oval. Spectator admission is free. Other things to enjoy for free include the Devonian Gardens, an oasis in the downtown core, and Prince's Island Park, a green space with hiking trails, playgrounds and skating rink. Locals enjoy the popular Calgary Folk Music Festival at the park.

How long to stay
If visiting for the Stampede, stay for a week or more to enjoy the shows; and make sure there's time to take in Calgary's other attractions.

What's nearby
Rosebud; Drumheller; Cochrane.

When to go
In summer catch the Calgary Stampede; Calgary is ideal for a winter visit, too, with numerous ski resorts nearby.

Hall of Fame, a tribute to the nation's best athletes. For skateboarders the downtown Shaw Millennium Skatepark has 7 hectares of skate surface. Cyclists can enjoy Calgary's 660 kilometres of pathways around the city.

Calgary has many green spaces including Fish Creek Provincial Park in the southern part of the city. This park stretches 19 kilometres from east to west along Bow River and Fish Creek. Wildlife is abundant here, and the great blue heron is a common sight. For more birdwatching visit Inglewood Bird Sanctuary, a 36-hectare reserve southeast of downtown. In the northwestern section is Nose Hill, an 11-square-kilometre park. A hike through the grasslands affords spectacular views over Calgary.

Heading West

AROUND COCHRANE AND TURNER VALLEY

For visitors to Calgary who want to escape the city for a day or for those who are starting a journey west of the city, there are a few small towns and hamlets close by that are worth either a day trip or one or two stops along the way.

Cochrane is northwest of Calgary, along the Bow River. Its serene setting is a draw for visitors to the area who can follow the paths along the river, catch a trout in one of the ponds or take in some genuinely warm hospitality at the old saloon. South of here is Bragg Creek, another friendly, western hamlet situated at the junction of the creek of the same name and Elbow River. Bragg Creek Provincial Park, just south of the village, is good for fishing.

Turner Valley, southwest of Calgary, was a hotspot when natural gas was discovered there in 1914, making it the birthplace of Alberta's oil and gas industry. However, more artists than oil barons now live in Turner Valley, drawn by its quiet charm and green, rolling hills. The Friendship Trail, a 3-kilometre paved path, winds along the Sheep River, linking Turner Valley with Black Diamond, to the east.

To appreciate ranching first-hand, visit the Bar U Ranch National Historic Site. Bar U celebrates this integral part of Alberta's past with rodeos, wagon rides and other activities, and it has a rich history of its own as a successful 19th-century cattle and horse ranch with visits by notorious outlaws such as the Sundance Kid.

Thrill ride The Elbow River by Bragg Creek is a popular kayak route, with a number of rapids for more experienced kayakers.

PLANNING

All three towns offer outdoor activities year-round, such as hiking and cross-country skiing. Near Cochrane is Ghost Lake, a popular sailing and ice-fishing spot.

CANMORE

The town of Canmore sits on the edge of the Rocky Mountains in the heart of the Bow Valley in the beautiful Kananaskis Country, a vast area of mountain and prairie scenery, glacial lakes and streams. Just an hour from Calgary, Canmore began as a coal-mining community in the late 1800s, and although it never attained the lofty reputation of

Cowboy Trail

Imagine following the path of 19th-century frontiersmen and cattle ranchers who rode through western Alberta. The Cowboy Trail is a 700-kilometre path along Highway 22, leading would-be cowboys from Cardston to Mayerthorpe through jaw-dropping mountain and prairie scenery. The trail leads through small western towns, such as Cochrane, and guided trail rides, wagon rides and other authentic experiences are offered. Many accommodation options are available, from rustic lodges to campgrounds and from relaxing guest ranches to working ranches, where visitors can be ranch hands during their stay.

Mountain hospitality Restaurants and galleries, some western themed such as The Settler's Cabin, line Canmore's welcoming main street.

its famous neighbour Banff, the town is a gateway to several provincial parklands, including Bow Valley, Peter Lougheed and Sheep River. Bow Valley's Many Springs Trail is the walk to take for its profusion of wildflowers and variety of birds. Peter Lougheed, at 4,200 square kilometres, is the largest of the parks, and its lakes, Upper and Lower Kananaskis, are ideal for anglers. Sheep River has 31 trails to hike and a wildlife sanctuary for bighorn sheep. A number of gentler walking trails, such as the Bow River Loop and Three Sisters Mountain Village Trail, can be found within the town of Canmore itself. More energetic visitors will be spoiled for choice with mountain biking, fishing, canoeing, rock climbing, ice climbing and caving, all of which are available in and around Canmore. To top it off, there's a good chance of spotting a moose during an early morning drive along Spray Lakes Road.

PLANNING
In winter visit Canmore Nordic Centre Provincial Park to cross-country ski at this venue built for the 1988 Winter Olympics. In summer take a helicopter ride over the area for amazing views of the Rockies.

🌲 👫 ♿ 🐦 ⛷ ⛵ 🎣

WATERTON LAKES
Bordering Glacier National Park in the U.S. state of Montana, this scenic wonderland often features in travel magazines because it epitomizes the Alberta landscape in so many ways. As a meeting point of ecosystems from north, south, east and west, Waterton Lakes National Park is a montage of mountain peaks, prairie grasses and glacial lakes. It is also home to cougars, grizzly bears, rare plants such as the moonwort fern, and fish such as northern pike. Waterton Lakes was appointed a biosphere reserve in 1979. Together, the American and Canadian parks form Waterton-Glacier International Peace Park,

Alpine glamour Tourists can travel the Great Northern Railway to stay at the Prince of Wales Hotel, a stately mountain chalet in a breathtaking location.

a sign of ongoing friendship between the two countries. In 1995 UNESCO designated the Peace Park a World Heritage Site.

Waterton's stunning natural attractions draw hikers, anglers, golfers, birdwatchers, skiers and other outdoor enthusiasts. However, its best-known, man-made attraction is a must-see, too. The Prince of Wales Hotel, a luxurious chalet-style hotel set on a bluff, was first opened in 1927. Even if the wallet can't stretch to the hotel fees, a visit to see this architectural gem will also be rewarded by the magnificent views of snow-topped mountains and turquoise lakes.

PLANNING
Ambitious hikers should try the Triple Crown Challenge to complete three strenuous hikes—Alderson-Carthew Summit, Crypt Lake and Akamina Ridge—in one summer. If you prefer a more leisurely pace, take a boat cruise through the park.

🌲 👫 🏛 ♿ 📷 🐦 ⛷ ⛵ 🎣

Scenic Journeys Around Banff

BANFF PARK

In 1885 Banff National Park became Canada's first national park, embracing some of Alberta's most dazzling locations: Banff, Lake Louise and Peyto Lake. The park's 6,600 square kilometres offer skiing, hiking, golfing, camping and fishing, as well as an old ghost town and luxury resorts. The town of Banff sits at the highest elevation in Canada and at the base of five rocky peaks, including Cascade and Sulphur Mountains. The Upper Hot Springs Trail is a forest path up Sulphur Mountain, leading to the hot springs and the gondola. A dip in the Upper Hot Springs is an exceptional treat, especially when the landscape is cloaked in snow. The Banff gondola goes to the summit of Sulphur Mountain to a lookout point over six mountain ranges. The complex includes dining facilities, gift shops and a picnic area. Back in town, the Fairmont Banff Springs Hotel, a late-19th-century building, strikes a dramatic pose against the mountain slopes and is just steps away from the main street. In addition to this grand accommodation, good restaurants, shopping and nightlife, Banff is known as an international arts hub. The Banff Centre hosts the Banff Summer Arts Festival, a celebrated annual event that features worldwide talent from all art forms, including dance, film, visual art, music and theatre. The Banff Park Museum National Historic Site is a natural history museum set in an early 1900s log building. On Birch Avenue is Buffalo Nations Luxton Museum, dedicated to the life and art of the Plains people.

Leave Banff for a leisurely drive north to Lake Louise, an alpine village set by a stunning lake of the same name. The lake is made even more breathtaking by the backdrop of Victoria Glacier. Hiking and skiing are popular pursuits here. The Icefields Parkway continues north to Bow Summit, overlooking Peyto Lake, a startling blue-green, glacier-fed lake. Particles of glacier sediment are responsible for the lake's

Turquoise dream A stunning view of Peyto Lake is a short hike from the Icefields Parkway. The lake was named for Bill Peyto, a mountain guide and park warden.

Glacial gem Originally called Emerald Lake, Lake Louise was renamed for Princess Louise, the daughter of Queen Victoria and wife of the Governor General.

brilliant colour. Farther north, Saskatchewan Crossing marks the confluence of the Howse, Mistaya and North Saskatchewan rivers. A viewing platform overlooks the valley and Howse Pass, an historic route through the Rockies from the eastern slopes to the Columbia Valley in the west.

PLANNING

Take a gondola ride. Gondolas travel up Mount Whitehorn for a bird's-eye view of Lake Louise and the surrounding area or go up Sulphur Mountain for views over Banff.

🌲 🏛 ⛷ 📷 🎿 🦅

JASPER PARK

Set in the Rocky Mountains of western Alberta, Jasper National Park is a wilderness paradise with more than 1,200 kilometres of trails, including multi-use and hiking trails, all types of campsites, waterfalls, lakes, forests and abundant wildlife. The town of Jasper, in the Athabasca Valley, is about half the size of Banff and retains its small town, alpine ambience. From here Jasper's natural wonderland is within easy reach. Jasper is a stargazer's delight. In March 2011 the Royal Astronomical Society of Canada officially designated Jasper National Park as a Dark Sky Preserve, making this 11,000-square-kilometre wilderness the largest such preserve in the world. Jasper is home to more than 50 species of mammals, including bighorn sheep, which are a frequent sight along Highway 16, woodland caribou, coyotes and grizzlies. Most of these large animals live in the montane region of the park, the forested valley. The Whistler's Tramway ascends 960 metres, past the montane region to the subalpine and finally to the alpine zone, where trees are stunted and plants such as the whistling marmot are the only ones to survive. One of the park's notable features is Maligne Lake, the largest glacier-fed lake in the

Rockies at 22 kilometres long and 97 metres deep. Pine and spruce forests surround the lake and tiny Spirit Island, a known beauty spot, lies in the middle. No road or trail leads to the island, but boat cruises take visitors nearby, offering a photo opportunity of the island and its surroundings. Jasper is also home to a lake that does a vanishing act. Medicine Lake appears in the summer when melt waters from the glacier fill the basin, but recedes when the waters drain into the lake's sinkholes. North of Medicine Lake, the Maligne River surges through the limestone canyon, with walls plunging more than 50 metres. The well-marked trail around the canyon is spectacular in summer or winter, and bridges provide amazing views.

PLANNING

The Dark Sky Festival runs in the autumn, with events and activities for everyone.

Glacier Highway

Traversing the tip of Banff National Park and the southern part of Jasper National Park, the Columbia Icefields encompass eight glaciers and covers 365 square kilometres. Many of the Rocky Mountains' highest peaks are in this glacial region. Glaciers are visible from the road or on helicopter tours, but to experience them up close climb on board one of the all-terrain vehicles and tour the Athabasca Glacier. The trip to the icefields is part of the experience, too. The 230-kilometre Icefields Parkway, Highway 93, passes a chain of icefields that border the Continental Divide, as well as Lake Louise, Mistaya Canyon and Peyto Lake, on its way to the Columbia Icefields.

Slippery climb Jasper has a number of ice-climbing routes in the Columbia Icefields area. The ice forms in drainage features where snow accumulates.

Enjoying Festive Edmonton

Alberta's capital city has matured into a thriving hub of arts, sports and entertainment, with at least 30 festivals every year. No wonder it's called Canada's Festival City.

Pioneer kitchen Historical re-enactments at Fort Edmonton bring to life everyday experiences in 19th-century Edmonton such as running a kitchen.

Edmonton began in the way of many Canadian cities: as a fort. The North West Company established Fort Augustus in 1795, while the Hudson's Bay Company set up Fort Edmonton nearby. The companies merged in 1821, abandoning Fort Augustus. The HBC moved the fort five times, finally settling on the land that is now Alberta's Provincial Legislature. From 1871 Edmonton's fortunes expanded, especially during the prosperous oil-boom era of the 1960s and '70s. Today, Edmonton is a modern, energetic city with a wide variety of attractions.

The Mall

West Edmonton Mall is not just a place for consumers, although with over 800 stores and 100 dining venues, it does qualify as an über shopping and eating destination. At almost 492,400 square metres, it is so large and its attractions are so many that it resembles a large, indoor resort. Visitors can even stay there because the mall has two hotels. It also has the world's largest indoor wave pool, a skating rink, bowling alley, amusement park and a replica of the *Santa Maria*, among other things. In the evening the mall's lively bars and casino fill with revellers.

Anchored history Visitors can board and explore this replica of the *Santa Maria*, moored in the West Edmonton Mall.

Festival City

At any time of the year Edmonton is alive with festival sights and sounds from jazz, blues and folk to dance, theatre and comedy. The Dreamspeakers Film Festival in late spring is a gala of Aboriginal filmmaking. In July the International Street Performer's Festival features more than 1,500 outdoor performances by entertainers and artists from around the world. This buoyant ten-day festival was the first of its kind when it started in 1984, and it is still one of the city's favourite celebrations. Also in July is the oldest running festival, Capital Ex, a ten-day Edmonton event with rides, concerts and other activities loved by visitors and residents alike. One of Edmonton's newest festivals is Metropolis, a salute to the best of winter, a season that the city embraces. Festivals take place in many parts of the city, including in Sir Winston Churchill Square, which hosts the Street Performers Festival and popular Christmas and New Year events. The Heritage Amphitheatre at William Hawrelak Park hosts the Free Will Shakespeare Festival and the Symphony Under the Sky.

History and natural beauty combine at Fort Edmonton Park in the southwestern part of the city. The 64-hectare park reconstructs four eras from Edmonton's past, beginning in 1846, at the height of the fur-trading years, and going on to pioneer days. Each period is imaginatively recreated as a living history lesson, enabling visitors to walk among the characters of the past and take part in a way of life long ago. See the fort as it would have been in the mid-1800s, then time travel to the schools and shops used by pioneers in 1885. From there, experience Edmonton when it became the province's capital in 1905 and continue to the 1920s street to see Canada's first mosque, built in 1938 and moved to Fort Edmonton. While there, stop at the old photographer's shop for an early 20th-century-style portrait. Throughout the summer season demonstrations and hands-on activities at each site provide entertainment and education, as do streetcars and amusement park rides. During the winter, the Capitol Theatre, a recreation of Edmonton's *circa* 1929 venue, provides a home for various productions.

River of steel The Art Gallery of Alberta's winding ribbon of steel reflects Edmonton's setting on the North Saskatchewan River.

Nature and Heritage

Edmonton's "Ribbon of Green" is the area of parkland that stretches 48 kilometres along the shores of the North Saskatchewan River as it runs through the heart of the city. There are 22 major parks by the river with more than 400 parks dotted around the urban area, making peace and quiet easy to find while exploring the city's sights. Cyclists, skaters, joggers and walkers make good use of the city's 160 kilometres of paved trails.

City Insider

Words to the wise
In the winter pack a warm parka to ward off the chill—temperatures average about -15°C from November to March—but also take sunglasses because, like much of Alberta, the sun shines brightly even in the colder months.

Locals love it
Skating at the large, outdoor rink at William Hawrelak Park is a favourite activity. After skating, sit by the outdoor fireplace and enjoy a cup of steaming hot chocolate.

How long to stay
A weekend in Edmonton is about right to enjoy some sights and take in the local scenery.

What's nearby
Elk Island National Park; Leduc; Fort Saskatchewan.

When to go
Events run throughout the year, so there is always something to enjoy. Winter and summer sports are a highlight of visiting the city. Due to its northern location, the summer days are long and warm, often staying light until 10 p.m. at night.

Don't Miss

Muttart Conservatory
Southeast of downtown, the conservatory's profusion of domestic and exotic plants are housed in an unusual building with striking architecture. Three of the conservatory's pyramids house a different biome: tropical, temperate and arid. The fourth pyramid displays temporary exhibits.

Art Gallery of Alberta
The province's art gallery is the oldest cultural institution in Alberta. A new building on Sir Winston Churchill Square is home to the gallery's collection, which features about 6,000 works, many by Western Canadian artists.

Whyte Avenue
This avenue is part of Old Strathcona, Edmonton's historic district and a separate town until 1912. Today, the area is full of boutiques, restaurants and bars that provide entertainment all day long.

ELK ISLAND PARK

Plains and wood bison, moose and elk roam the aspen parkland that make up Elk Island National Park, located less than an hour away from Edmonton. In 1906 the government created Elk Park to protect the small herd of 75 elk in the area, and the park still takes an active role in elk conservation. Unlike any other national park, high fencing surrounds Elk Island, an unusual feature that protects the park's mammals from outside predators such as bears and wolves. Diverse trails, including some on floating boardwalks, wind through ponds and lakes, provide numerous opportunities to observe wildlife such as grebes and pelicans, beaver, bison and moose. The elk can be difficult to spot, especially during the day, but winter provides some sightings. Heritage sites within the park are few but include the Ukrainian Pioneer Home, which is the oldest purpose-built Ukrainian museum in Canada.

Day Trips Around Edmonton

DEVONIAN GARDEN

Just west of Edmonton, the Devonian Botanic Garden, part of the University of Alberta, is an idyllic setting for a day out of the city. The garden takes up almost 77 hectares, with bountiful displays of roses and peonies as well as structured gardens and greenhouses. Featured gardens include Plants of Alberta, the Herb Garden, the Primula Dell and the Alpine Garden. The Native People's Garden leads visitors into an area where plant names appear in Latin, English and Cree. Cactus, agave and other desert plants fill the Arid Plant House, and bougainvilleas climb up the Tropical and Sub Tropical Plant and Butterfly Greenhouse, where butterflies flutter around orchids and hibiscus. The Kurimoto Japanese Garden, a meditative space designed in traditional kaiyou style, features stone lanterns, a belfry and a pagoda.

PLANNING

Lovely throughout the summer, a visit in the spring is especially fragrant and an ideal time to see the gardens awaken.

🌲 ⛩

Oil!

On February 13, 1947, oil gushed from the Leduc #1 well, near Edmonton, ending a dry spell for Imperial Oil, which had drilled 133 wells between 1912 and 1947, none of which had yielded any oil. Seismic testing had revealed an odd rise in the underlying formation, prompting Imperial's chief geologist to recommend Leduc as a drilling site. Drilling began in November 1946, but it wasn't until it reached 1,544 metres that the #1 well struck liquid gold. This changed the course of Alberta's history. Today, visitors to the Leduc #1 Energy Discovery Centre can visit the site of the well, and learn how a drilling rig operates and about the development of Alberta's oil industry.

PLANNING

In spring visitors may spot the orange hue of the bison calves, while in autumn they may see birds migrating south, which use Astotin Lake as a staging area.

UKRAINIAN VILLAGE

Just outside Elk Island National Park is the Ukrainian Cultural Heritage Village, an open air museum that chronicles the story of the Ukrainian immigrants who settled the area between 1892 to 1930. Most immigrants worked the land, and the museum reflects this with the farmstead zone and costumed workers who lend authenticity to the scene. In the rural community area are homesteads, barns, a sawmill and roadside shrine while a blacksmith shop, lumber company and livery barn are some of the structures that create the townsite. In addition, two simple, country churches grace the rural area. These

Roaming bison Trails in Elk Island National Park take hikers past wood bison. This mammal, classified as threatened, is protected at this and other parks.

Festive dancers Young women at the Ukrainian Cultural Heritage Village wear traditional "vinoks," colourful floral garlands tied with ribbon.

resemble those that early settlers would have built, while the more elaborate St. Vladimir's Church in town represents the church of the later, more prosperous community. To create the museum, more than 30 structures were moved to the area, restored and then furnished in the style of the period.

PLANNING

The museum is 50 kilometres east of Edmonton, making it an easy day trip. In May the village comes alive with Ukrainian music and festivity in the Celebration of Dance.

STURGEON COUNTY

The area north of Edmonton is dotted with small towns such as St. Albert, Bon Accord and Gibbons, each offering a friendly welcome to travellers. St. Albert, just outside of Edmonton, is home to Musée Héritage Museum, which traces the area's past from

its beginnings as a mission and highlights the contributions of the town's Métis and francophone residents. In Gibbons walk part of the Trans Canada Trail's northern path along the Sturgeon River, formerly used by freight wagons in the late 1800s. You can also visit the Jurassic Forest, a preserve set in an old growth forest, and dig for fossils. Gigantic, lifelike dinosaurs await brave explorers. For more family entertainment, head to Westlock to the Canadian Tractor Museum, for tractor pulls and shows, and the Pioneer Museum, a small gallery housed in an old swimming-pool building.

PLANNING

The trails in Jurassic Forest are closed in winter, as is the Pioneer Museum at Westlock. Tours at the Tractor Museum are year-round, although shows are seasonal.

DINOSAUR HUNTING IN ALBERTA

When dinosaurs roamed Alberta 75 million years ago, the landscape was subtropical, but this changed with the last ice age, when the melting glaciers formed the hoodoos and mesas of today's badlands. Since the first fossil discovery in 1884, fossil hunters have taken more than 300 well-preserved skeletons from the area within Dinosaur Provincial Park. The Royal Tyrrell Museum in Drumheller has one of the largest displays of fossils in the world.

Planning:
Don't attempt to visit both the Royal Tyrrell Museum and the park in the same day. They are two hours apart, and there is a lot to see at both places.

FORT MCMURRAY

Situated at the confluence of four rivers, Fort McMurray began as a fur-trading post and became the town centre of the world's largest, single oil deposit, the Athabasca Oil Sands. The Heritage Museum highlights the town's past, while the Oil Sands Discovery Centre celebrates its present. The museum's historical buildings range from 1911 to 1940, encapsulating that period in Fort McMurray's history. The Discovery Centre goes back in time to the Aboriginal people who used oil to seal their canoes and forward to the methods used today to extract the oil. Before the 1920s Fort McMurray was only accessible by water, and canoeing is still a popular pastime through the boreal forest along the picturesque Clearwater and Athabasca rivers.

Superfruit The Saskatoon berry is native to Grande Prairie and some other parts of Canada. The berries are flavourful and rich in antioxidants.

Northern Alberta

GRANDE PRAIRIE

The large visitor's centre on the Highway 43 bypass greets travellers to Grande Prairie, in Alberta's Peace Country, and this is a good place to start when exploring the region. The town began as a fur-trading post and missionaries followed, naming the town after its sprawling, open landscape.
The Grande Prairie Pioneer Museum in Muskoseepi Park reconstructs a 19th-century village with a post office, church and school among other buildings. Saskatoon Mountain, west of the city, rises 945 metres and offers great views of the surrounding farmland and small towns. Just west of the city is Saskatoon Island Provincial Park, a place for camping, hiking and picking Saskatoon

berries. Most significantly, in summer it is also the spot to see the endangered trumpeter swan from the viewing platform on Little Lake. A little farther out is Kakwa Wildland Park, an area of beautiful kettle lakes, pine and spruce forest and mountain peaks. Hiking trails lead to the Kakwa River, which drops 30 metres over Alberta's highest waterfall, Kakwa Falls.

PLANNING

Visit in April for the Swan Festival at Saskatoon Island Provincial Park. In summer Grande Prairie hosts a rodeo, while nearby Teepee Creek hosts one of the oldest stampedes in Canada.

🌲 🏛 🦢

If hoping to catch the wondrous sight of the aurora borealis, the best time to go is between October and March. Between December and April, ice fishing is at its best.

🏛 🛶 🐟

ATHABASCA

The town of Athabasca is approximately 145 kilometres north of Edmonton on the shore of the Athabasca River. The Hudson's Bay Company founded Athabasca Landing at the southern loop of the river, and established the Athabasca Landing Trail for portaging from the North Saskatchewan River. Few buildings remain from Athabasca's past, but the old train station, the schoolhouse and United Church are examples of its early architecture. One fascinating historical nugget is the story of the Amber Valley settlement. In 1910 a few African-Americans moved to the area just east of Athabasca, fleeing racism and persecution in Oklahoma. At its peak, Amber Valley comprised about 300 residents, but most people had gone by the 1930s to seek their fortunes elsewhere. Similarly, Keystone, near Edmonton, underwent the same pattern. The rugged, sometimes unforgiving land around Athabasca has challenged many pioneers, but today's sightseers can enjoy its natural beauty. A trail travels along the Tawatinaw Valley, with many birdwatching spots along the way. Lakes, including Baptiste and Island just west of the town, surround Athabasca, and are favourite fishing and camping spots. Muskeg Creek Trails are 17 kilometres of wilderness-like hiking and cross-country ski trails right in the town. Near the trail is the Athabasca University's NASA Northern Lights Station.

PLANNING

Visit in the spring and summer to enjoy the area at its best.

🐦 🎿 🛶 🐟

River hunt The Peace River Valley is home to rare birds of prey such as the bald eagle. The river provides abundant supplies of fish.

PEACE RIVER

Northern Alberta's Peace River Country surrounds the long, powerful river that winds through aspen parkland in this part of the province. Anglers fish the river for walleye and northern pike. Use the town of Peace River as a base for exploring this remote region. To the south Sagitawa is a spectacular lookout point and picnic spot that offers views of the town and river from Judah Hill. The scenic Shaftesbury Trail runs along the west side of the river for more than 25 kilometres. Winagami Lake Provincial Park is a birdwatcher's wonderland, with a viewing platform where visitors can spy on more than 200 species of waterfowl and songbirds. Part of Peace Country's early history is captured at the Dunvegan Provincial Park, east of Peace River. Built on the site of an early 1800s trading post and mission, the park features restored log buildings and market gardens cultivated as they would have been in the 19th century.

PLANNING

The best fishing is in May and June. Canoe rentals are limited; bring your own if you can.

🌲 🏛 🐦 🐟

Island playground MacDonald Island Park, in Fort McMurray between the Clearwater and Athabasca rivers, has an entertainment complex and golf course.

A Dozen Great Places to Ski in the West

Whistler Blackcomb, Whistler B.C.

Canada's most famous resort, which played host to the Winter 2010 Olympics, is a top destination for skiers from all over the world. The Whistler and Blackcomb Mountains are part of B.C.'s Coast Mountain range, north of Vancouver. The resort offers more than 200 marked trails and over 3,000 hectares of powder paradise. It consistently wins awards as one of North America's top skiing destinations. Whistler's varied terrain means there is something for novices, families, experts and everyone in-between. The Highest Level, on Blackcomb, has a 146-metre vertical drop and offers an exhilarating challenge for advanced skiers, as do the heli-skiing and snowboarding excursions and amazing off-piste opportunities. The town of Whistler is just the spot for après-ski, with its great dining

Other Great Places to Ski

Banff, Banff National Park, Alberta. In Banff, with one lift ticket, there is a choice of three resorts: Sunshine Village, Lake Louise and Norquay. Lake Louise is the largest with runs such as the steep, tight Gravity Pull.

Marmot Basin, Jasper, Alberta. This relaxed resort in Jasper National Park lays claim to the highest base elevation in Canada. The Canadian Rockies Express carries skiers up almost 600 vertical metres.

Mount Washington, Courtenay, B.C. Vancouver Island's Mount Washington has more than 450 hectares of varied ski terrain. Its towering presence between the Pacific Ocean and Strait of Georgia means deep, ample snow. Backcountry skiers can head to Strathcona Provincial Park.

Fernie Alpine Resort, Fernie, B.C. Fernie's terrain offers steep chutes such as the runs between the Currie and Lizard Bowls and double black diamond Siberia Ridge. Wide, groomed trails are ideal for beginners.

Kicking Horse, Golden, B.C. Kicking Horse is not for the timid. Its upper mountain has three separate bowls with steep chutes, although the resort does have some wide cruisers near the base of the mountain.

Sun Peaks, Kamloops, B.C. Sun Peaks is a large resort spread over Tod and Sundance mountains and Mount Morrissey. Tod tests advanced skiers with the Challenger Run and deep, powder-filled bowls, while Sundance's gentler slopes are best for beginners and intermediates.

Big White, Kelowna, B.C. About half the area is good for intermediate skiing at this family-friendly resort, but the Parachute offers a challenge for the advanced skier with its near-vertical, treeless open bowl. Beginners can take lessons at Big White's excellent school.

Whitewater, Nelson, B.C. Deep, light powder—more than 12 metres a season—and the legendary backcountry draw passionate skiers to Whitewater, in the high alpine bowl of Ymir Peak. The Glory Chair takes skiers to awesome glades and views of the Kokanee Glacier.

Panorama Mountain Village, Panorama, B.C. With wide cruising runs, a vertical of 1,220 metres and its Extreme Dream Zone, Panorama suits beginners to experts. Afterwards, the Panorama Springs Hot Pools, the largest slopeside hot pools in Canada, are a welcome sight for weary skiers.

Revelstoke Mountain, Revelstoke, B.C. At 1,713 metres, this resort in the Selkirks offers the greatest vertical in North America. The North Bowl is a favourite for deep powder, but there are also new beginner areas.

Red Mountain, Rossland, B.C. Great tree skiing and powder distinguish this laid-back resort. The resort's steep terrain is challenging, from the Red Towers to the cliff drops and gullies on Granite Mountain. The resort's "ski anywhere" policy is a huge attraction for backcountry skiers.

and lively nightlife. Like a northern Sundance, Whistler's winter film festival is just another reason to head to this vibrant resort.

Planning: The peak-to-peak gondola offers extraordinary views, especially from within the glass-bottom cabins and provide a quick way to get from one mountain to another.

Eastern British Columbia

YOHO NATIONAL PARK

In Cree, *yoho* is an expression of awe, a perfect description of the stunning Yoho National Park comprised of glacier-fed lakes, rugged Rocky Mountain peaks, tumbling waterfalls and streams. Yoho sits on the western slopes of the Continental Divide and borders Banff National Park to the south. From a viewpoint on the highway, see the innovative Spiral Tunnels wind in and out of the mountains. They were built in the early 1900s for the railway and are still in use today. More than 400 kilometres of trails in the park lead to other wonderful sights.

Beginning at the Hoodoo Creek Campground, a short but steep trail leads to the strange-looking hoodoos, pillars of glacial debris. Guided hikes lead to the fascinating Burgess Shale fossil beds. The fossils are the remains of an ancient marine ecosystem that flourished in the area about 505 million years ago, in the Middle Cambrian period. The most amazing fossils are well-preserved, soft-bodied marine organisms, a significant

Alpine lake A fragile beauty, Lake O'Hara is framed by stunning, rocky peaks. An extensive network of trails surrounds the lake.

Rockies Passage

The construction of the Canadian Pacific Railway helped bring settlers and prosperity to western Canada and to join British Columbia with the rest of the nation. Creating passes through the mountains proved challenging, and the Selkirk Mountains seemed the last major obstacles to continuing the railway line west. Major A.B. Rogers found the narrow pass that bears his name, and the railway constructed a line through it, using the passage from 1885 until 1916. However, avalanches, mudslides and thick snowfall plagued the railway line, causing many deaths and much damage, and forcing the company to close the track. The Connaught Tunnel, which runs underneath the pass, took its place, and now the Trans-Canada Highway, which used much of the original railbed, passes through the area, surrounded by stunning mountain scenery.

Winter wonderland Nelson provides a warm welcome to visitors who come to ski at nearby Whitewater, one of Canada's top ski resorts.

feature of the Burgess Shale. There are two hikes that will take you to the fossils: a long, taxing trek leading to Walcott's Quarry and a shorter, but strenuous hike to Mount Stephen fossil bed. At almost 250 metres high, Takakkaw Falls are the third highest in Canada. The waters cascade into the Kicking Horse River, which has carved a natural, rocky bridge. Many think the crowning glory of Yoho is the pristine, alpine beauty of Lake O'Hara, a deep, turquoise-coloured lake surrounded by meadows and mountains. Located near the village of Field, a bus or hike takes visitors to this protected area.

PLANNING
Reserving guided hikes to the fossil beds is strongly recommended, although standby spots are sometimes available at the last

minute. The hikes are not suitable for children under eight years of age.
♣ ⛩

NELSON
This former silver-mining town is a well-preserved Victorian gem by the edge of the western arm of Kootenay Lake and surrounded by the Selkirk Mountains. Nelson has more than 350 heritage buildings in its downtown core and in the surrounding residential areas. A walk along Baker Street is a step back in time architecturally, although the buildings now house excellent stores and restaurants. Another old-time treat is a ride on the town's restored streetcar.

After the mining boom, Nelson's next round of settlers included draft dodgers from the United States, who sought refuge from the Vietnam War in the 1960s and '70s. Many stayed, bringing a new energy to the small town. Nelson is known as an arts centre, supporting many musicians and artists in the community. The Touchstones Nelson Museum of Art and History celebrates Nelson's long and ongoing connection with the arts, as does the restored Capitol Theatre.

Outside of town, nearby activities include skiing, golfing, hiking and swimming. Eight provincial parks are within a short distance, as is the long stretch of Kootenay Lake and the Whitewater Ski Resort just a short drive from downtown Nelson.

PLANNING
Throughout the summer, stores and restaurants in downtown Nelson transform into galleries for the ArtWalk, showing the works of numerous, talented local artists.
♣ 🏛 🖼 ⛷

Mineral bath The water at Radium Hot Springs has been associated with health benefits for centuries, but the first concrete pool was not constructed until 1914.

KOOTENAY PARK
The Banff-Windemere Highway, which opened in 1922, was the first motoring road through the Rocky Mountains, meandering along the Vermillion and Kootenay rivers through to Radium Hot Springs. At the same time, the provincial and federal governments agreed to set aside 8 kilometres on either side of the highway, now known as Kootenay Parkway, as Kootenay National Park. The park, located south of Yoho, is distinguished by its natural diversity, which ranges from high, glacial mountains to grasslands where cactus grows. The Ktunaxa (Kootenay) and Kinbasket (Shuswap) First Nations used the park as hunting grounds many years ago. Today, travellers through the park can spot bighorn sheep, especially in the winter when they come to the valleys in search of food. At the southern end of the Kootenay Parkway, just outside the park, is Radium Hot Springs, whose natural mineral pools are surrounded by walls of rock.

PLANNING
Before going on an overnight backcountry hike, purchase a Wilderness Pass from the visitor centre. Reservations are recommended.
♣ ⛩

HAIDA GWAII

The stunning archipelago of Haida Gwaii, which means "island of the people," is the traditional and contemporary home of the Haida Nation. Around the islands are ancient and modern villages, remarkably preserved totem poles and longhouses, as well as abundant wildlife, some of which are unique to Haida Gwaii. Gwaii Haanas National Park Reserve protects much of the cultural and natural heritage of the islands.

The Heart of B.C.

KELOWNA

Carved by glaciers, the Okanagan Valley is a series of fertile valleys in south-central British Columbia bordered by the Monashee Mountains to the east and the Cascades to the west. Kelowna, on the eastern shore of Okanagan Lake, is probably best known as the centre of the wine and orchard country, but the city itself is a vibrant place with fine restaurants, art galleries and accommodations from which to plan an Okanagan adventure. While in the city, two galleries worth exploring are the Geert Maas Sculpture Gardens and Gallery, which features over 350 works, and the Kelowna Art Gallery, a modern space that showcases contemporary Canadian artists. With the wilderness its backyard, Kelowna is popular for outdoor activities, in and outside of the town. At Lion Park, watch salmon spawning from mid September to mid October, head to Hot Sands Beach in City Park for a walk on the boardwalk or to Waterfront Park for sailing. For hiking and horseback riding, Okanagan Mountain Provincial Park, just south of Kelowna, is an ideal spot, as is Myra-Bellevue Provincial Park, where walkers can follow the historic Kettle Valley Railway Trail. Kelowna also boasts the longest, driest golfing season in Canada and some of the country's best courses.

PLANNING

In July the Kelowna Regatta takes over Okanagan Lake. In winter skiiers can choose from four ski resorts including Big White that are a short drive away from the city.

PENTICTON

The name means "a place to live forever," and many people would agree that Penticton deserves this accolade. The weather is mild, the sun shines most days and the city sits between Okanagan Lake and Skaha Lake, within some of the country's most beautiful scenery. Most people come to Penticton to enjoy the outdoors, whether to rock climb the Skaha Bluffs or hike the Carmi/Ellis Creek Trail. In the summer Penticton has a choice of sandy beaches on both lakes, providing ideal spots for swimming, windsurfing and lake cruising. Come winter hit the slopes at Apex Mountain or try cross-country skiing. While in the area, visit the pretty towns of Summerland and Naramata, just north of Penticton. Summerland is famous for its Tudor-style main street, but while there ride

Scenic journey From Lillooet, a railway shadowed by soaring mountains runs to Seton Portage along the edge of Seton Lake.

on the 1912 steam train and journey along the only preserved section of the old Kettle Valley Railway. Naramata's charms include the Manitou Beach, less busy than Penticton and great for families.

PLANNING
Visit during the fall wine festival; it takes in Penticton and other Okanagan Valley towns.

🌲 🏛 ⛵ 🎿 🚣

OSOYOOS
The Okanagan First Nations' name, Osoyoos, describes the town's setting alongside where Osoyoos Lake narrows as "a place the land almost meets." Osoyoos is the Okanagan Valley's southernmost community and a border town, sharing its lake with the U.S. state of Washington. Its position at the northern tip of the Great Basin Desert means Osoyoos' climate is dry and hot in the summer and mild in the winter. The Okanagan's oldest vineyards are here, their founders taking advantage of the ideal grape-growing climate. The lush landscape contrasts with Canada's only pocket desert, in northwest Osoyoos. Here, in this fragile

ecosystem, an elevated boardwalk winds around the bunchgrass and prickly pear cacti. Osoyoos' Aboriginal history comes to life at Nk'Mip Desert Cultural Centre in the desert hillside. The centre features a reconstructed Okanagan village and trails through the sage grassland and pine forest. Near to town, water activities are popular on the lake, as are biking and hiking on the International Hike and Bike Trail that follows the Osoyoos River. Anarchist Mountain Lookout provides views of the Okanagan Valley, or climb Mount Kobau, one of the area's tallest peaks.

PLANNING
See the rare burrowing owl, a prairie falcon and numerous birds in the Osoyoos Oxbows Wildlife Management Area along the Okanagan River channel.

🐦 🦅 🐟

Nk'Mip greeting A large, metal sculpture welcomes visitors to the Nk'Mip Desert Cultural Centre. Indoor and outdoor exhibits celebrate this Aboriginal nation.

LILLOOET
In the mid-1800s, the gold rush town of Lillooet was one of the largest cities west of Chicago. The Chinese Rock Piles along both shores of the Fraser River were piled there by the immigrants who came to search for gold. Before that, the Sek'wel'wás people lived in pit houses built in the hillsides. A guide takes visitors to a replica pit house. When the prospectors arrived, Lillooet became the starting point of the Cariboo Road that continued to Barkerville. Mile "O" Cairn, a monument in the centre of town, commemorates the old wagon route. Today, people come for the trails and fish rather than for gold. However, Lillooet also has rich deposits of nephrite jade, and there are over 30 jade monuments dotted around the town.

PLANNING
In fall catch the salmon run on the Lillooet River or fish for sturgeon on the Fraser. Lillooet hosts the Sturgeon Fishing Derby in summer.

🏛 ⛵ 🎿 🐟 🐟

WINE TASTING IN BRITISH COLUMBIA

Planning:
Other top regions for wine tasting include Vancouver Island and the Similkameen Valley, both with more than ten wineries to visit. The wine-touring season runs from April until October, but off-season visits may be available by appointment.

There are more than 200 wineries in British Columbia
producing over 60 varietals. The Okanagan Valley, with its
hot, dry summers, is the province's major wine-producing area.
Award winning Pinot Gris, Gewürztraminer, Merlot and Syrah
are just some of the vintages to be enjoyed at the wineries
scattered along the length of the valley.

Exploring Scenic Vancouver

Set between mountains to the east and the Pacific Ocean to the west, Vancouver is perfectly positioned as the crown jewel of British Columbia's coastline.

All cities have their own vibe, and Vancouver is no exception. Distinctly west coast in its relaxed ambience, Vancouver is also a brilliant mosaic of art and culture, natural splendour and metropolitan sophistication.

The Old and the New

Gastown, downtown near Vancouver Harbour, lays claim to be the city's birthplace. A sailor called John "Gassy Jack" Deighton opened a tavern here in 1867, and people soon followed. This is still a good place to stop for a beer and people-watch, amble the cobbled streets and shop for Aboriginal art or local designer wear. The world's first steam-powered clock is Gastown's centrepiece and a Vancouver landmark. Steam powers the clock and pours out of the top once an hour, marking the time with whistling toots.

Yaletown, south of downtown by False Creek, is another revitalized district. A former garment district full of warehouses, Yaletown is now a trendy area with the added bonus of the adjacent waterfront. Steveston, a former fishing village and important seaport, is now a community in the southwest of the city on the Fraser River. The old canneries form an historic site, but Steveston is still Canada's largest commercial fishing harbour—and the place to board a boat for whale-watching.

City by the sea With towering buildings in the background, parkland, beaches and marinas border Vancouver's cityscape, making much of the waterfront easily accessible.

Native treasures Galleries in the Museum of Anthropology showcase about 6,000 elaborately carved totems, canoes and other Aboriginal objects.

Vancouver's roots lie in the history of the Coast Salish Nation. Archaeological evidence found around the city establishes the presence of Squamish, Sliammon and other Aboriginal people about 8,000 years ago. Some of this evidence is on exhibit at the city's Museum of Anthropology, set on the western edge of the city, overlooking the Salish Sea. The museum, part of the University of British Columbia, sits on traditional Musqueam First Nations land. The building's design mirrors a traditional northwest coast structure, its towering

Don't Miss

Dr. Sun Yat-Sen Chinese Garden
Established in 1986 as the first authentic Chinese garden outside of China, the space represents the traditional gardens of the Ming dynasty in which scholars would live and work. The careful arrangement harmonizes the core elements of plants, rocks, water and architecture so they reflect the balance of yin and yang.

Commercial Drive
"The Drive" is a hip, young neighbourhood with a variety of global dining choices. After the Second World War, a wave of Italian immigrants settled in the area that is now known as "Little Italy." The ethnic mix has grown, but there is still a strong link with the area's Italian past.

Canada Place
White sails line the top of Canada Place, which juts out like an ocean liner into the harbour. Take a walk along the promenade for views over the water. Also, depending on the season and for special city events, the sails light up at night in a colourful display of graphics and light.

Vancouver Art Gallery
The gallery in downtown Robson Square is housed in a former neoclassical courthouse built in 1906. Courtrooms have been modernized to hold exhibits such as the best of B.C. artist Emily Carr and work by international photographers.

glass walls and wooden beams providing an expansive space in which to view its thousands of objects from B.C.'s First Nations' people and other parts of the world.

Cultural Kaleidoscope
Vancouver's many cultures imbue the city with vibrancy and diversity. The city's Chinatown is one of the largest in North America and serves as a focal point of Vancouver's considerable Chinese population. Enter through the China Gate on Pender Street and visit the Chinese Cultural Centre Museum. In the evening go shopping in the night market. The Chinese Festival takes over the streets in the summer. Japanese culture is also represented at the

City Insider

Words to the wise
Commuters use the SkyTrain during rush hours, but in between, this light-rapid transit is a great way to travel around the city.

Locals love it
Lynn Canyon Park, in North Vancouver, is the place to picnic and swim. The park's 50-metre-high suspension bridge spans a scenic canyon and provides amazing views of the river and falls.

How long to stay
Plan to visit for no less than a long weekend to walk part of the Seawall, wander Gastown and pop into Stanley Park.

What's nearby
Gulf Islands; Gibsons; Harrison Hot Springs.

When to go
Sports lovers will find plenty to do in winter and summer. Festivals during the year include the International Jazz Festival in late June to early July and the Celebration of Light in late July to August.

beautiful Nitobe Memorial Garden, near the Museum of Anthropology on Point Grey. Set near the botanical gardens of the University of British Columbia—also well worth a visit—the Nitobe Garden features an authentic Tea Garden and Tea House. Japanese festivals include Sakura Days Japan Fair, the springtime Vancouver Cherry Blossom Festival and the Powell Street Festival, a community fête celebrating Japanese arts.

The Indian community converges at the Punjabi Market, a neighbourhood along Main Street, and not a market as such. Come here to savour the best curries and indulge in some shopping for spices or silk. Catch the Diwali Festival in late autumn for a celebration of dance, music and light.

A Breath of Fresh Air

Trails, water and snow sports, gardens, mountains and sea are so much a part of the fabric of Vancouver that there seems little separation between the two. A case in point is Stanley Park, a 404-hectare oasis at the tip of the peninsula. It's easy to spend an entire day here with so many activities on offer. Marvel at the totem poles at Brockton Point, breathe in the fragrance of water lilies on Beaver Lake, wander through the arboretum of the Shakespeare Garden, take the kids on a miniature train ride and go beluga-watching at the aquarium. If that's not enough, go to the beach, try for par at the pitch and putt or cycle the paths. Vancouver's seawall is a 22-kilometre, paved pathway running along the city's waterfront from Coal Harbour, through Stanley Park and on to Kitsilano Beach. Run, cycle or walk along the seawall for a truly authentic Vancouver experience.

From Stanley Park, the Lions Gate Bridge Road stretches across the Burrard Inlet to North Vancouver and leads to more of the city's main attractions. One of Vancouver's best-loved treasures is the 70-metre-high Capilano Bridge, which has a 130-metre span over the Capilano River. The site has been attracting tourists since the late-19th century, but the bridge is now made of reinforced steel in place of wood and rope. The bridge is part of a park to which admission is charged. Other attractions in the park include the Cliffwalk around the edge of Capilano Canyon and the Treetops Adventure, an interconnecting series of bridges set high above the forest floor, the Totem Park, and Kia'palano, a First Nations museum.

The Burrard Street Bridge links the downtown peninsula with Kitsilano, one of Vancouver's hippest neighbourhoods. Called "Kits" by locals, the area owes its

Beluga show This popular attraction at the Vancouver Aquarium in Stanley Park offers a rare opportunity to see these beautiful white whales.

Mountain lookout In the winter Grouse Mountain stays open after dark, so skiers have spectacular views of the downtown lights.

name to Xats'alanexw, a Squamish chief. The neighbourhood boasts two beaches on the shore of English Bay. During the summer Bard on the Beach is a popular outdoor theatre event in Vanier Park.

Farther north is Vancouver's Grouse Mountain, reaching 1,231 metres at its summit. Its proximity to the city centre is a boon for skiers, hikers, skaters and zip-lining enthusiasts. Visitors can buy day passes to enjoy various activities depending on the season. The SkyRide, an aerial tramway, takes sightseers up the mountain year-round, where they can overlook the city, the Pacific and nearby peaks. In winter they can bring ice skates to glide on the mountaintop pond or enjoy an old-fashioned sleigh ride. Or visitors

across False Creek, especially since parking is difficult. The Public Market is the hub of the island where shoppers can browse through stalls displaying artisan cheeses, baked goods, fresh produce, jewellery, glasswork and more. Outside the market food stands, cafés and restaurants tempt the taste buds, while street performers and artists' studios attract the eye. The Emily Carr University of Art and Design, on Granville Island, exhibits the works of up and coming artists. The Kids Market, next to the Public Market, caters to the younger crowd, and the large water park is the perfect place to cool down and burn off some energy. There is free, outdoor theatre to enjoy and a rock cave to explore, not to mention getting out onto the water in a kayak or a boat from one of the marinas.

Live entertainment is part of the Granville Island experience, with theatre and festivals throughout the year such as Vancouver International Fringe Festival and the Wooden Boat Festival. Catch a show at the Waterfront Theatre or where the Arts Club Theatre Company performs.

Emily Carr

Although Emily Carr began her artistic career early on, it wasn't until her fifties that she began painting the canvases for which she is best known. Born in Victoria in 1871, Carr travelled to San Francisco and Paris to study art, but returned to Canada in the early 1900s. After trips to document the culture of B.C.'s First Nations, she spent several years alienated from her art until a meeting with Lawren Harris of the Group of Seven in 1927 changed all that. Harris encouraged Carr to return to British Columbia and paint the landscapes that inspired her and in a style that she would claim as her own. Deep colours, bold brush strokes and mystical Aboriginal imagery infuse Carr's most striking paintings.

can try out the ski slopes or rent snowshoes for a slow-paced or vigorous hike, depending on which of the four trails they choose. Not included in the day pass is the Eye of the Wind, a tour that takes people to the top of a 20-storey-high wind turbine for spectacular 360-degree views. Not for the faint of heart, the Grouse Grind is a gruelling, 2.9-kilometre, steep hike up the mountain face. The climb is a favourite with locals, who've dubbed it "Mother Nature's Stairmaster."

Arts Island

Although it's not technically an island, travelling to Granville Island from downtown is a good excuse to take the Aquabus or a ferry

Market shopping Locals and visitors flock to Granville Island's market to shop for an amazing variety of fresh food, arts and crafts.

Coastal and Island Trips from Vancouver

GIBSONS

At the southern edge of B.C.'s Sunshine Coast, the town of Gibsons lies just across Howe Sound from metropolitan Vancouver. A slice of life from long ago, this tranquil, seaside setting is far removed from the big city. Salmon fishing, sailing and walks along the shore are everyday occurrences rather than merely a weekend treat. Captain George Vancouver landed nearby during his epic 1792 voyage of discovery, but it was another hundred years before George Gibson and sons pioneered the site, never dreaming that their town would win a UN-backed competition in 2009 for "most liveable community under 20,000." Seafood restaurants and art galleries gather around the boat-filled harbour. The nearby Sunshine Coast Museum & Archives provides insight into the local culture and natural history.

The Sunshine Coast's gorgeous scenery continues north of Gibsons, with notable stops at Roberts Creek, a quaint village with ocean views; Sechelt, the gateway to some of the world's best coldwater diving; and Desolation Sound Marine Provincial Park, where sailboats glide in and around the bays and coves.

PLANNING

The annual Sea Calvacade Carnival, salmon fishing derbies and outrigger canoe races make summer the best time to visit.

HOPE

Flanked by sheer mountains and set at the confluence of the Fraser and Coquihalla rivers, Hope has been a busy crossroads and meeting place since the Hudson's Bay Company founded a fur-trading post here in 1848. Nowadays, this town has several offbeat claims to fame. Canada's self-appointed "chainsaw carving capital" has a competition every year. More than 30 large wooden sculptures, hewn by gas-powered blades, decorate spaces around the town. Near Hope, in the Coquihalla Canyon Recreation Area, wander through the Othello Quintette Tunnels, five passageways designed by an early-20th century engineer for the Kettle Valley Railway. The tunnels cut through the Coquihalla Canyon, but rock slides and washouts besieged the railway line and it was abandoned in 1959. Several spectacular bridges, such as the suspension bridge in Alexandra Bridge Provincial Park, span the canyon, high above the whitewater

Hollywood North

British Columbia has earned the moniker "Hollywood North" for the numerous well-known productions filmed in the province's towns and wilderness parks. Seaside towns such as Gibsons take the place of New England villages, while urban Vancouver stands in for American city scenes. Movies and television shows made in B.C. include *Charlie St. Cloud*, *The A Team*, *Twilight Saga: New Moon* and much of *Eclipse* and *Breaking Dawn*. The long-running television show, *Smalltown*, was filmed in and around Vancouver, as well as the more recent *Once Upon a Time*.

gorge. A journey along Highway 1 also provides dramatic views of the canyon.

PLANNING
Adventure sports are popular in the summer months, but fall brings the best fishing in the Fraser River and the Brigade Days, an autumn celebration of early pioneer life.
🌲 ⛰ 🐟

Canyon trail Trains once steamed through the Othello Quntette Tunnels, but pedestrian pathways have replaced the old tracks through the Coquihalla Canyon.

SOUTHERN GULF ISLANDS

Nearer Vancouver Island than the city, regular ferries travel to and between these picturesque islands. The largest and most popular is Salt Spring, the scenic home to an art-oriented, patchwork community of musicians, painters, writers, organic farmers, artisan bakers and others. Ganges is the island's main town, and Centennial Park is the site of its most visited attraction—the large, open-air Saturday market. The market runs from spring until autumn and features a variety of local and organic food, flowers, art and crafts. "Make it, bake it, or grow it" is the market's slogan, and everything for sale there has been grown or made on the island.

Outside of Ganges, a wealth of natural escapes beckon. Ruckle Provincial Park, in the southern part of Salt Spring, and Mount Maxwell Provincial Park, in the centre, both offer extensive networks of trails and beaches for outdoor explorers, scuba divers and birdwatchers. Baynes Peak in Mount Maxwell is one of the highest points on the island, where climbers are rewarded with stunning views.

Less populated, the remaining Gulf Islands are ideal for hiking, kayaking, diving or discovering a secluded beach. See the rock formations at Bellhouse Provincial Park on Galiano and the curved limestone, called the Malaspina Galleries, on Gabriola. Almost half of Saturna Island is part of the Gulf Islands National Park Reserve; however, one of B.C.'s largest vineyards is also here, offering tastings as well as lunches and dinners through the summer season.

PLANNING
Summer is the best time for island hopping. Visit the artists at work on a self-guided studio tour of Salt Spring. Download or pick up a brochure and map as a guide to more than 30 studios around the island.
🌲 ⛴ ⛰ ⛵ 🐟

Natural sculpture Soft limestone is easily carved by the forces of nature, as witnessed in this formation on Gabriola, one of the Southern Gulf Islands.

Touring Vancouver Island

VICTORIA

The elegant city of Victoria is Vancouver Island's largest urban community and the province's capital. Situated on the island's southern tip, it was a strategic location for the Hudson's Bay Company's Fort Victoria. Established in 1843, and named for the British queen, it became a crown colony in 1849 and part of British Columbia in 1866.

The Inner Harbour is the heart and oldest part of the city, where structures such as the regal provincial parliament buildings and Edwardian-style Empress Hotel helped to formalize Victoria's importance in western Canada. During this time wealthy industrialists made their homes in the city. One the most famous of these homes is the elaborate Craigdarroch Castle, which was built by coal baron Robert Dunsmuir, who didn't live to see its completion.

These days double-decker buses, tearooms and pubs give an affectionate nod to the city's British past. However, modern Victoria has more diverse cultural offerings and an abundance of outdoor recreational opportunities right on its doorstep. Water surrounds Victoria on three sides, making marine adventures almost synonymous with a stay in the city. It's the home of Canada's Pacific Naval Fleet, a sailing centre, a fishing capital and a launching port for cruises and whale-watching. One of the best diving spots in the world, Ogden Point Breakwater is just a stone's throw from where the cruise ships dock.

Still in the Inner Harbour and close to the parliament buildings, the Royal BC Museum includes the fascinating First Peoples Gallery, an evocative look at Aboriginal culture in B.C. before and after the arrival of Europeans. Nearby the Modern History Gallery contains reconstructions of a homestead and a 19th-century streetscape, as well as other explorations of the province's human and natural history. Close to the Inner Harbour are two distinctly different parks. Beacon Hill Park, which was established in 1882, features ponds and paths winding through groomed gardens. Totem poles, a longhouse and other structures populate Thunderbird Park, creating a striking outdoor art gallery.

Several attractions are within a short drive from downtown Victoria. Butchart Gardens, about 23 kilometres north, is one of the island's best-loved parks, set in a former quarry. In the early 1920s Jennie Butchart, the quarry owner's wife, started the garden after the pit's closure and transformed the unlikely space into a splendid sunken garden. Northeast of here, on the Saanich

Victorian luxury The regal Empress Hotel, which opened in 1908, overlooks Victoria's Inner Harbour. The hotel serves traditional afternoon tea in an elegant lobby.

Pacific Rim National Park Reserve

This exquisite park on the west coast of Vancouver Island encompasses areas of temperate rainforest, intertidal and subtidal zones. The park is home to an array of wildlife, including green anemones and starfish in the tide pools and oystercatchers on rocky outcrops. Three units comprise the park: the 16-kilometre strip of land between Tofino and Ucluelet, called the Long Beach Unit; the Broken Group Islands Unit, an archipelago of more than 100 islands and rocks; and the 75-kilometre West Coast Trail Unit, which runs north from Port Renfrew to Bamfield. The Long Beach Unit is the most accessible for beach walks, trails, camping, fishing and surfing, while in good weather kayakers can paddle around the rocky shores of the Broken Group Islands. The West Coast Trail lures fit and experienced backcountry hikers to test their endurance, with entrance points at Pachena Bay in the north and Gordon River in the south.

Peninsula, is the little seaside town of Sidney. Here, the Shaw Ocean Discovery Centre is an excellent place to explore the area's marine life. Strathcona Provincial Park, in the centre of Vancouver Island, is a 250,000-hectare haven of mountains, lakes, waterfalls and forests of cedar and fir.

PLANNING

Go to Victoria for the International Yacht Race in May or the Classic Boat Festival, which takes place over Labour Day weekend.
🌲 🏛 🖼 ⛵ 🐦

TOFINO

Nestled in Clayoquot Sound Bay on Vancouver Island's western shore, Tofino is a small resort town popular with artists, surfers, whale-watchers and sightseers. Surprisingly, before the 1970s, Tofino's allure went relatively unnoticed by most of the world, except for the Nuu-chah-nulth First Nation, who had lived and prospered here for thousands of years, followed by a few fishermen, loggers and surfers in the 20th century. This changed in 1971, when the government established the Pacific Rim National Park Reserve, protecting the strip of land along the shore as well as the islands in Barkley Sound. Visitors began arriving at Tofino to enjoy its ocean setting and explore the beautiful surroundings. Much of Tofino's appeal is its embrace of nature and Aboriginal culture. Tofino's Botanical Gardens is a mix of shoreline, forest and gardens interspersed with art installations and winding paths. Boat tours take visitors to Hot Springs Cove, north of Tofino, to walk through the cedar forest and see waterfalls, hot spring pools, seals and sea lions. Other tours go to Meares, Flores and Echachist Islands. Back in town, Tofino hosts a number of festivals through the year such as November's Clayoquot Oyster Festival.

PLANNING

Whale-watch from March to April, when 17,000 grey whales migrate past Tofino to their summer home in the Arctic.
🌲 🖼 ⛵ 🐦

Catching waves Tofino's location on the Pacific makes it a surfer's paradise. Chesterman Beach is ideal for beginners, while Cox Bay has larger swells for more skilled surfers.

A Dozen Great Golf Courses in the West

Fairmont Jasper Park Lodge, Jasper National Park, Alberta

Renowned architect Stanley Thompson designed this lush course, carving it into the Rocky Mountains. Thompson created the course in the UNESCO Heritage Site of Jasper National Park in the 1920s, using the mountains as dramatic focal points at many holes, and winding wide, green fairways through Jasper's thick forest. Elevated tees offer staggering views of the parkland beyond and the bunkers mimic the shapes of the snow-topped peaks. In the 1990s restoration work refurbished some of Thompson's original plans, including the bunkers and tees. The golf course is known for its variety of holes, some of which Thompson designed with a quirky sense of humour. The ninth, called Cleopatra, is a curvy hole in keeping with its name and is the course's signature hole. The 14th near Lac Beauvert is the beginning of three holes around the peninsula, and it requires a challenging shot off the tee

Other Great Golf Courses

Fairmont Banff Springs, Banff, Alberta. Banff Springs offers one of Alberta's best golfing experiences in the heart of the Rockies. Sulphur Mountain and Mount Rundle overlook the course.

Stewart Creek, Canmore, Alberta. Framed by the Three Sisters peaks, Stewart Creek features lush fairways between rocky outcrops and pine trees. Sculpted over old mine shafts, with some entrances added to the design, the course presents a challenging experience from the very first hole.

Kananaskis Country, Kananaskis, Alberta. This 36-hole complex is an easy drive from Calgary. Robert Trent Jones Sr. designed the two courses: Mount Lorette, which features water, and Mount Kidd, which has more sand. The courses are named for the mountains that overlook them.

Wolf Creek, Ponoka, Alberta. Rod Whitman designed Wolf Creek in the Scottish tradition, making the most of its sand-belt location to create two fabulous 18-hole courses.

Westwood Plateau, Coquitlam, B.C. Michael Hurdzan designed this stunning course on the Coquitlam plateau east of Vancouver. The course slopes and rises around Eagle Mountain and features a helipad so golfers can arrive in celebrity style.

Crown Isle, Courtenay, B.C. Vancouver Island's golf course, designed by Graham Cooke, has splendid views of the Beaufort Mountains and features 11 lakes.

Gallagher's Canyon, Kelowna, B.C. As its name suggests, this William Robinson-designed, championship course sits on the edge of a canyon, giving golfers astounding views over the Okanagan Valley.

Big Sky, Pemberton, B.C. Settled at the base of Mount Currie, north of Whistler, is this 6,500-metre course designed by Bob Cupp. The link design incorporates seven lakes connected by a winding creek.

Radium Resort Springs, Radium Hot Springs, B.C. Radium boasts two courses set within the Columbia River Valley between the Purcell Mountains and the Rockies. Both have breathtaking scenery, but the Springs, designed by Les Furber, presents the most challenges, including the 6th, with its collection of bunkers, and the 17th, a par three over a gorge.

Predator Ridge, Vernon, B.C. British Columbia's Okanagan Valley makes the ideal setting for Predator Ridge's two courses. The Ridge Course has spectacular views over Lake Okanagan.

Nicklaus North, Whistler, B.C. This course, designed by golf legend Jack Nicklaus, is a golf course to please and challenge players of all abilities. Views of the Coast Mountains make Nicklaus North a beautiful setting in which to drive and putt.

to carry the ball over the lake and around the trees. The 18th is a long, downhill par four leading neatly into the 19th, for a well-earned drink at the clubhouse or more luxurious Emerald Lounge.

Planning: If staying in the area, enjoy the pleasures of Jasper National Park and compare Fairmont Jasper Park Lodge with Banff Springs, another Thompson-designed golf course.

Northern British Columbia

BARKERVILLE

This former gold-rush town is still bustling, but no one has lived here for years. Instead, the spirits of the first prospectors live on through actors who play them and other people from the town's past. The town is named for Billy Barker, who found gold in Williams Creek in 1862. Many people followed, looking for similar fortune. They journeyed from Quesnel to Barkerville on the Gold Rush Trail, often stopping at the Cottonwood roadhouse along the way. Today, this preserved site still offers refreshment to modern-day travellers on the trail. Within this reconstructed town, 100 restored buildings are original to Barkerville. The town's authentic structures and objects include those in its reconstructed Chinatown, which exhibits one of the largest Chinese archival collections in Canada. In the summer the actors play out events from Barkerville's pioneer days. There are lessons in the schoolhouse and stagecoach rides, gold panning, theatre productions at the Theatre Royal and four general stores from which to buy wares. If staying near or in the town, a trip to Bowron Lakes Provincial Park makes a change of pace. The large wilderness park is renowned for canoeing and worth a longer stay for skilled paddlers. There are easy walking trails near the lake.

PLANNING

Special events are held in summer, including Gold Panning Championships in August; the town is closed for part of the winter.
👫 🏛 ⛵

PRINCE GEORGE

The North West Company founded Fort George in 1807, naming it for Britain's King George III. In 1915 the town was incorporated as Prince George, possibly named for the Duke of Kent. Today, B.C.'s "capital of the

Frontier winter Snow may cover Barkerville's historic buildings from late autumn to spring. The town hosts an annual Victorian Christmas celebration.

TWEEDSMUIR PARK

The expansive wilderness in Tweedsmuir Provincial Park covers 981,000 hectares, about half of which, in North Tweedsmuir Park, have limited access. However, Highway 20 goes through the middle of South Tweedsmuir Park, and from there, hiking, canoeing, fishing and portaging is the way to explore. A few day trails such as Burnt Bridge are short treks and a good way to get a taste of this awe-inspiring backcountry. Alexander Mackenzie explored the territory in 1793, and experienced hikers may wish to tackle the strenuous, month-long hike named in his honour. The Hunlen Falls Loop Trail leads to one of Canada's highest waterfalls, where water cascades 260 metres from Turner Lake over a sheer rock face. Another remarkable feature of the park is

Ghost Towns

Towns sprang up all over British Columbia during the feverish mining and gold-rush years. Hopeful settlers arrived to work or seek their fortunes, but as mines closed and gold was less easy to find, people deserted the towns, which fell to ruins. Some such as Barkerville and Fort Steele have been revived as heritage sites, while many others such as Anyox in northwestern B.C. lie abandoned, sad and eerie remnants of a more optimistic time.

the Rainbow Range, comprised of brilliantly coloured volcanic peaks, stained red, yellow and purple through thousands of years of weathering and oxidation.

PLANNING

Grizzlies and black bears roam the park, so visitors are cautioned to be aware, especially by the Dean, Atnarko and Bella Coola rivers, where the bears fish for salmon.

north" is a vibrant community with many attractions within and outside the city. The Exploration Place in Fort George Park provides a tour of the past, from prehistoric times to the present through the Paleontology Galleries, the First Nations Gallery and the Sports Hall of Fame. Stargazers will enjoy a trip to the Prince George Centre Observatory for spectacular views of the night sky. The Railway and Forestry Museum is a good introduction to two of Prince George's main industries. For a lively history lesson, Fort St. James, 160 kilometres north of Prince George, is restored to its 1896 period. Buildings include the Officer's House, where visitors can book a stay for a 19th-century, overnight experience. Within driving range of Prince George are Evanoff Provincial Park and Close To The Edge Provincial Park, both with excellent caving opportunities.

PLANNING

Prince George is a year-round destination, with popular winter and summer sports.

Wilderness tranquillity At close to a million hectares, Tweedsmuir is one of B.C.'s largest provincial parks. Its unspoiled waters are ideal for canoeing and fishing.

the
NORTH

The Yukon

TOMBSTONE

Named after the gravelike Tombstone Mountains, Tombstone Territorial Park is 56 kilometres due east of Dawson along the Dempster Highway. Tombstone is remote, but it has a number of distinct ecosystems such as pingos and palsas—strange dome or ridge-shaped permafrost landforms—and a wide variety of northern flora and fauna. Grizzly Creek Trail is the only established hiking route; otherwise, visitors need the aid of compass and map or GPS.

PLANNING

The Tombstone Interpretive Centre is open from May 20 to September 15. Nearby is the park's only organized campground, but there are also three primitive backcountry camping sites in the region. Reservations and permits are required, available at the visitor centre.

WHITEHORSE

Tucked beneath steep cliffs on the western bank of the Yukon River, Whitehorse is both the capital and southern gateway to the Yukon Territory. Protected by the palisades and nearby Big Salmon Mountains, the climate is warm compared to elsewhere in the north. Stampeders on their way to the 1890s Klondike gold rush camped in the riverside flats beneath White Horse Rapids. The town was founded in 1900 when the White Pass & Yukon Railway terminated at the same spot, transforming Whitehorse into a strategic transfer point for prospectors and goods headed down the river. More than a century later, the city still has a boom-town vibe. Some gold-rush structures have endured, most notably the Old Log Church (1900) and several log "skyscrapers" along Lambert Street. The Klondike stampede and pioneer times are the central themes of the MacBride Museum. Alternatively, go back to prehistoric times at the Yukon Beringia Interpretive Centre, which revolves around the giant mammals and cave-dwelling humans of the last ice age. Summer is the season for outdoor recreation (hiking, biking, kayaking, fishing, camping), but February brings the Sourdough Rendezvous, Frostbite Music Festival and Yukon Quest dogsled race. The White Horse Rapids are

Stunning landscape Tombstone is located in a transition zone between boreal forest and tundra.

174

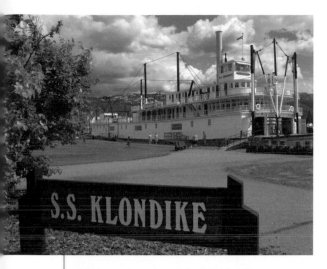

Whitehorse Step aboard the S.S. *Klondike*, an original Yukon sternwheeler launched in 1936 and now a floating museum.

Mount Logan

Towering above Kluane National Park and Reserve, Mount Logan (5,959 metres) is Canada's loftiest point and has the second highest peak In North America. It is named for Sir William Logan, who founded the Geological Survey of Canada (GSC). Active tectonic uplifting means the mountain's elevation is constantly rising. The current height was established by a 1992 GSC expedition. Even more impressive is the mountain's bulk: it has the largest circumference of any non-volcanic mountain on the planet. A 20-kilometre-long glaciated plateau covers the top of the mountain.

KLUANE

One of Canada's largest and wildest wilderness reserves, Kluane National Park and Reserve embraces nearly 22,000 square kilometres of mountain—including Mount Logan (see left)—forest, ice fields and waterways in the Yukon's southwest corner. Along with adjacent parks in Alaska and British Columbia, Klaune forms part of the world's largest internationally protected wilderness area and is a UNESCO World Heritage Site. The majority of the park is inaccessible to anyone but the most intrepid hikers and mountaineers. The alternative is "flight-seeing" trips or short day hikes at Soldiers Summit, Rock Glacier and Kathleen Lake. Haines Junction is the hub for helicopter or bush-plane excursions over the park, as well as the starting point for Kluane mountaineering and whitewater raft trips along the wild and remote Alsek River.

long gone, replaced by Schwatka Lake and its hydroelectric dam. You can view chinook salmon bypassing the dam via the world's longest wooden fish ladder from an observation deck at the end of Nisutlin Drive.

PLANNING

Courtesy of tourism and its ongoing role as a transportation hub, Whitehorse is easy to reach by plane, train and motor vehicles.

combine with other cold-weather recreations such as cross-country skiing, ice fishing, snowmobiling, lake skating and skiing or snowboarding on Mount Maichen.

PLANNING

Watson Lake is astride the Alaska Highway near the British Columbia border, making it a destination or stop along the route.

PLANNING

The park's only drive-in campground is at Kathleen Lake, but it's open year-round for winter camping. There is a national park visitor centre at Haines Junction.

WATSON LAKE

Watson Lake is a small mining and logging community with a large First Nation population. Residents know exactly where they are thanks to Sign Post Forest, with more than 50,000 signs representing cities and towns all around the globe. The first sign, for Danville, Illinois, was erected by homesick American GI Carl Lindley in 1942. Watson Lake is well-situated for viewing the aurora borealis in wintertime, when the skies are clear and the nights are long. The high-tech Northern Lights Space & Science Centre explores the myth and physics of the aurora borealis as well as the Canadian space program. Aurora-borealis viewing is easy to

Wildlife haven Dall sheep are silhouetted against a blue sky in Kluane National Park and Reserve, which is also home to mountain goats, caribou, moose, black bears and grizzly bears.

Gold Rush Days in Dawson City

At the turn of the 20th century, this Yukon riverfront town and its rich gold fields attracted a stream of miners intent on getting rich quick.

Not many people would have settled in the northern Yukon in the 1890s, but the presence of shiny yellow flakes in the local soil and riverbeds was a magnet for the would-be miners and frontier entrepreneurs who founded Dawson City. The initial discovery of gold was made by three friends— George Carmack, Tagish Charlie and Skookum Jim—who came across gold nuggets along a tributary of the Klondike River in the summer of 1896. The discovery set off a stampede of thousands of miners into the region, mostly by way of Skagway, Alaska, and a dangerous overland route that took many lives.

Dawson City sprang up at the confluence of the Klondike and Yukon rivers. Although some of the miners struck it rich, the people who really made a profit were the town's saloon and dance-hall owners, brothel madams and hoteliers, who were paid in gold by the miners. Dawson City's population peaked at about 30,000 people at the turn of the 20th century. However, when the gold fields started to run dry, the population plunged, and Dawson appeared to be headed for the same ghost-town fate expierenced by many other gold rush settlements, until the Canadian government decided its history was too rich to squander.

Exploring the Old Town

The Dawson Historical Complex National Historic Site embraces several locations in the Dawson City area, including eight

Boom town Dawson City's carefully restored historic structures are the main attraction on bustling Front Street.

square blocks of downtown where the bulk of stampede-era buildings are located. Among the architectural relics are the former Territorial Court House (1901) and its trademark copula, and the Gothic revival-style, yellow brick St. Andrews Church and Manse (1901). The S.S. *Keno* sternwheeler is permanently tied to the Dawson waterfront, built in 1922 for service on the Yukon River and now a floating museum. To the left of the boat, the imposing Canadian Bank of Commerce building's classical frontage is made not of sandstone but of pressed metal painted

Mail Race! This annual event is in honour of Percy DeWolfe, who delivered mail in all weather for 30 years.

Don't Miss

Diamond Tooth Gertie's
This vintage saloon and gambling hall on Queen Street—named after one of the gold-rush era's more colourful characters—tenders nightly music and floor shows. All proceeds from gambling are channelled into historic renovation.

Palace Grand Theatre
Guides in vintage costumes spin tails of stampede days in this pinewood playhouse built by "Arizona Charlie" Meadows in 1899.

Jack London Cabin
American author Jack London's stay in the Klondike lasted less than a year, but he immortalized the region in books such as *Call of the Wild*. This is a replica of London's 1897 cabin.

Robert Service Cabin
The Canadian poet Robert Service ("Bard of the Yukon") lived in this two-storey home from 1909 until 1912, working as a bank clerk while he was honing his verse. There are daily readings of his poetry during the season.

to look like stone. From 1898–1908 the bank processed $44 million worth of gold. The Dawson City Museum, housed in an elegant Victorian building, details the history of the Klondike Gold Rush.

The Tr'ondëk Hwëch'in First Nation people, who occupied the Klondike for thousands of years prior to the gold rush, are the focus of the new Dänojà Zho Cultural Centre, which is located on the waterfront.

The Parks Canada Visitor Information Centre on Front Street is open May–September and provides information on these sites. You'll also find information on a number of year-round activities such as The Yukon River Quest—the longest annual kayak and canoe race—and arts and music festivals.

City Insider

Words to the wise
Parks Canada's daily pass includes tours of the Dawson Historical Complex, S.S. *Keno* and Dredge No. 4, as well as entry to the Dawson City Museum and Dänojà Zho Cultural Centre.

Locals love it
During the off season (October–April) the town fades back into its uncrowded, unrushed, end-of-the-world alter ego.

How long to stay
Dawson City can be toured in one long day, but two days are recommended

for those who want to discover more about the local history.

What's nearby
Tombstone Territorial Park; Top of the World Highway; Klondike Highway; Dempster Highway.

When to go
Many of the historical attractions and activities are open only during the summer season from May through September. However, there are several cold-weather events in Dawson City, such as the Percy DeWolfe dogsled race and mail run in March.

Finding Gold

The 1896 gold was found in a placer field—an area of mineral deposits in a stream bed—at Bonanza Creek, 15 kilometres up from its confluence with the Klondike, and the area is now preserved as the Discovery Claim National Historic Site. A trail details the history of the rush and the story of the stampeders who flocked there. Visitors can handle genuine equipment along the trail.

Parks Canada has also preserved Dredge No. 4 as an example of the corporate mining of the Klondike gold scene later in the 20th century. The huge 8-storey-high mechanical contraption worked Bonanza Creek from 1912 to 1960, when it was retired. It was the largest of its type in North America.

A Dozen Great Scenic Drives in the North

Driving the Alaska Highway

The Alaska Highway stretches 2,237 kilometres from Dawson Creek, British Columbia, to Delta Junction, Alaska. It cuts a scenic swath across the southern Yukon via Watson Lake, Whitehorse and Haines Junction. The route (also known as the Alaska–Canada Highway, or Alcan) is taken by many travellers as much for its remarkable history as for its stunning forest, lake and mountain landscapes.

Although most of the route passes through Canadian territory, the U.S. government agreed to fund the construction of the road during the Second World War to create a supply route between Alaska and

the other U.S. states, away from the turbulent—Japanese submarine-filled—Pacific. Working from both ends, construction crews completed the route in just seven months, from March to October 1942.

Nobody could have foreseen in those days that the Alaska Highway would be transformed into one of Canada's most renowned tourist attractions. Although now completely paved, driving through the northern wilderness on a two-lane highway where you can go hours without seeing another vehicle still feels like an adventure. On the mountainous sections you might find yourself driving by caribou or stone sheep, while in the valleys moose may wander onto the highway.

Other Great Drives

Dempster Highway, Dawson City, Yukon, to Inuvik, Northwest Territories (735 kilometres). Canada's northernmost public road shoots due north into the tundra.

Haines Highway, Haines Junction, Yukon, to Haines, Alaska (244 kilometres). Follows an ancient trade route over Chilkat Pass to the sea.

Ingraham Trail, Yellowknife to Tibbitt Lake, Northwest Territories (70 kilometres). Made famous by the U.S. television series *Ice Road Truckers*, this remote route threads the boreal forest north of Great Slave Lake.

Klondike Highway, Dawson City, Yukon, to Skagway, Alaska (705 kilometres). Drive in days the route that often took the stampeders months to cross.

Liard Highway, Fort Nelson, British Columbia, to Fort Simpson, Northwest Territories (138 kilometres). This remote, often unpaved route is the only road between British Columbia and the Northwest Territories.

Mackenzie Highway, Grimshaw, Alberta, to Wrigley, Northwest Territories (1,155 kilometres). This gateway to the Northwest Territories took more than 50 years to build.

Nahanni Range Road, Tuchitua, Yukon, to Tungsten, Northwest Territories (196 kilometres). This "back door" into Nahanni National Park Reserve is one of Canada's most remote roads.

Robert Campbell Highway, Watson Lake to Carmacks, Yukon (583 kilometres). This mostly gravel route provides access to the western end of the Canol Heritage Trail near Ross River hamlet.

Top of the World Highway, Dawson City, Yukon, to Tetlin Junction, Alaska (282 kilometres). Highland route that is only open May to October.

Tuktoyaktuk Winter Road, Inuvik and Tuktoyaktuk Northwest Territories (194 kilometres). Winter-only ice road across the Mackenzie River Delta to a secluded settlement on the Arctic coast.

Yellowknife Highway, near Fort Providence to Yellowknife, Northwest Territories (380 kilometres). This route around the west end of Great Slave Lake starts with a ferry or ice road across the Mackenzie River.

Along the 1,387-kilometre drive between Dawson City and Whitehorse, you'll cross the Rocky Mountains and drive through wide valleys. Drivers can stay overnight in campgrounds or motor hotels and lodges along the route. Service stations can be 160 to 240 kilometres apart, so keep an eye on the needle gauge for your fuel tank.

Planning: *The Milepost* (www.milepost.com) offers updated information on road conditions and accommodations along the route. Make reservations for room accomodations or if using the ferries on either end of the route; early September has fewer people—and insects—and is good for autumal colours.

The Northwest Territories

WOOD BUFFALO

Sprawling across the frontier between the Northwest Territories and northern Alberta, Wood Buffalo National Park takes its name from the herd of bison that roam this secluded park. The park is also noteworthy as the only nesting spot of the rare whooping crane and as a refuge for other at-risk species such as the wolf and the peregrine falcon. The flat landscape is broken by three rivers (Athabasca, Slave and Peace), a large freshwater delta and geological oddities such as salt flats and karst rock formations. Fort Smith in the north and the remote Fort Chipewyan in the southeast are the two gateways to the park. Wood Buffalo summers are ideal for canoeing, camping and hiking; winter activities include cross-country skiing, snowshoeing and watching the aurora borealis.

PLANNING

The Mackenzie Highway provides year-round access to Fort Smith, which has campgrounds and day-use areas off Pine Lake Road. Fort Chipewyan is only reachable by air or boat in the summer and by land in winter.

YELLOWKNIFE

The copper knives traded by the region's Dene people gave the city its name, but gold mining turned Yellowknife into a boom town in the 1930s. Mining is still important in this capital city, but diamonds are the focus since the last gold mine shut in 2004. Almost one quarter of the population is First Nation, and many of the 20,000 residents speak indigenous languages. Yellowknife is divided into two sections. Dating from the gold rush, Old Town hugs a peninsula stretching into the lake. Among its icons are the Wildcat

Cafe, Gold Range Hotel and Bush Pilot's Monument. The New Town is dominated by the modern Northwest Territories Legislative Building and the Prince of Wales Northern Heritage Centre, with its excellent displays on the Dene, Inuit and other northern cultures.

PLANNING
Visit between mid-June and mid-July for outdoor activities and festivals, including the Midnight Classic Golf Tournament and the Folk on the Rocks music fest.

🏛 🛶

FORT PROVIDENCE

Located near the junction of the Yellowknife and Mackenzie highways, Fort Providence lies on the north bank of the Mackenzie River not far from Great Slave Lake. It is largely populated by First Nation Dene. The area is rich in natural attractions. Lady Evelyn Falls plunges over a crescent-shaped cliff 56 kilometres to the south. East of town, where the lake empties into the Mackenzie, is leafy Fort Providence Territorial Park. North of town is the Mackenzie Bison Sanctuary and its 2,000-strong buffalo herd.

PLANNING
Fort Providence hosts an annual Mackenzie Daze celebration, a weekend event in August with cultural activities and canoe races.

🌲 🛶 ⛵

NAHANNI

After tumbling over 92-metre-high Virginia Falls, the Nahanni River cuts a deep path through four gorges in the southwest corner of the Northwest Territories. Sometimes called the Grand Canyon of Canada, the huge trough in the Nahanni National Park Reserve can be reached only by foot along

remote hiking routes or whitewater river trips that last from one to three weeks. Beyond the canyon walls, the reserve unfolds into a huge stretch of wilderness with aspen and spruce forests and impenetrable mountains. Sites at Virginia Falls and Glacier Lake are ideal for picnics and hikes into surrounding woods.

PLANNING
Located east of the park, the visitor centre at Fort Simpson is a good place to stage excursions. Or book a "flight-seeing" trip from Fort Smith or nearby towns, or a day trip by float plane to Virginia Falls or Glacier Lake.

🌲 ⛵

NORMAN WELLS

Reached only by plane or boat, Norman Wells lies more than 160 kilometres down the Mackenzie River from Fort Simpson. The town's name betrays its history of oil extraction. A relic of that era is the Canol Heritage Trail, which follows the old 372-kilometre pipeline route between Norman Wells and the Yukon. Hiking the trail can take a month, but a long day hike is

enough to get a feel for the boreal terrain. The Norman Wells Historical Centre highlights the area's natural and human heritage.

PLANNING
Daily flights from Yellowknife and Inuvik go to Norman Wells. The Sahtú Wilderness Centre offers advice for canoe and hiking trips in the local wilderness areas.

🌲 🛶 ⛵

Nahanni Lakes and hot springs provide stunning scenery with mountains forming the background.

Nunavut

ARVIAT

Located on the western shore of Hudson Bay, Arviat is the southernmost town in Nunavut, the federal territory carved out of the Northwest Territories in 1999. With exhibits on local history, nature and Inuit life, the Margaret Aniksak Visitor's Centre doubles as the town museum. Just offshore are Arvia'juaq Island and its hundreds of archaeological sites dating back to the Thule period 900 years ago. More than a quarter million feathered creatures find a temporary home each summer in the nearby McConnell River Bird Sanctuary. Along with the Iditarod in Alaska, the Hudson Bay Quest each March is one of the world's top dogsled races. The 400-kilometre race stretches between Arviat and Churchill, Manitoba. The other big annual events are the Hamlet Days and Inuumariit Music Festival, which are combined in September.

PLANNING

One of the easiest town to reach in Nunavut given its transportation links (airplane, boat or snowmobile, depending on the season) to Churchill. Arviat offers safaris by dogsled, snowmobile and ATV (all-terrain vehicle) as well as hunting and fishing.

BAKER LAKE

As Nunavut's only inland community, Baker Lake affords a rare opportunity to explore the interior Arctic. Founded as a Hudson's Bay Company Trading Post in 1916, the community has grown as a result of nearby mining and increasing tourism. A thriving arts community, Baker Lake is known for its weavers, sculptors and printmakers. Their work is displayed around town. The town is also a jumping-off point for canoe and kayak expeditions across the lake and nearby heritage rivers such as the Kazan and Thelon. Arctic wildlife is abundant, especially in the Thelon Wildlife Sanctuary west of Baker Lake, where musk ox, caribou, grizzly bear and wolf roam. Each autumn the migrating caribou have crossed the Kazan River along a shallow stretch of water between Kazan Falls and Thirty Mile Lake. This Canadian national historic site commemorates both the ever-wandering animals and the Inuit who hunted them from kayaks.

PLANNING

Located in the Hudson's Bay Store/Trading Post, the Vera Akumalik Visitor Centre offers advice on how to explore the region.

Harpooning The Inuit have perfected their hunting skills to cope with the frozen conditions in the Arctic.

REPULSE BAY

"Resting Place for Seagulls" (*Naujaat*) is the Inuktitut name for Repulse Bay, and the community lives up to the appellation as a summer gathering place for thousands of waterfowl (gulls, loons, eider ducks) that nest on the cliffs north of town. The Arctic Circle runs through the hamlet, commemorated by a stone arch. Repulse Bay is also the gateway to Ukkusiksalik, a recently established national park (in 2003) that wraps around the coast of Wager Bay. The park is one of the best places in the Arctic to get a close-up view of a wide variety of large animals, including polar bear, narwhal, caribou and wolf. Ukkusiksalik is also rich in archaeology, with more than 500 sites stretching from the Paleolithic Thule and Dorset cultures (around AD 1000) to the early 20th-century presence of the Hudson's Bay Company.

PLANNING
The best place for wildlife viewing is Sila Lodge on the north shore of Wager Bay in

Fire and Ice Sea ice glows rose gold in the light of the setting sun on Wager Bay.

Dog mushing Teams of dogs pulling a sled are a traditional form of transportation still used by the Inuit today.

the heart of Ukkusiksalik National Park. The lodge, which operates from early July to late August, is reached by boat or float plane from Repulse Bay.

GJOA HAVEN

This tiny coastal community on King William Island played a huge part in the search for the Northwest Passage and the magnetic north pole, as well as being the place where famed polar explorer Roald Amundsen was stranded for nearly two years (1903–1905) waiting for the Arctic ice to thaw. In fact, the hamlet is named for his ship, the steel-hulled *Gjoa*. The area is also associated with Sir John's Franklin "lost expedition" of 1845–46, during which all hands perished and the last survivors turned to cannibalism. The history of local polar exploration plays out in placards and sights along the Northwest Passage Territorial Trail, which meanders in and around Gjoa Haven. Gjoa Haven's 9-hole Central Arctic Coast Golf Club is one of only a handful of places where golfers can tee off above the Arctic Circle (summer only, of course). Sports fishing and wildlife-watching excursions are options, too.

PLANNING
There are no roads to the island. Flights are available from Cambridge Bay, Kugaaruk, Taloyoak and Yellowknife.

KUGLUKTUK

Perched at the place where the Coppermine River flows into the Coronation Gulf, Kugluktuk ("Place of Moving Water") is the westernmost town in Nunavut. The town is a hub of government and transportation for the territory's Kitikmeot region, as well as an important centre for Inuit art and culture. Kugluktuk residents usher in the spring with the Nattiq Frolics, a week-long festival of song, dance, food and traditional activities, both old and new such as the Mr. and Mrs. Coppermine contest. Upstream is Bloody Falls Territorial Park: the cascade takes its name from a 1771 massacre of Inuit families by Dene warriors.

PLANNING
Kugluktuk Heritage Centre is the place to learn about local history and activities such as summer river trips on the Coppermine.

THE NORTHERN LIGHTS

An aurora is a natural light display in the sky in the high latitude (Arctic and Antarctic) regions, caused by the collision of energetic charged particles with atoms in the high altitude atmosphere (thermosphere). Those in the north are called aurora borealis, or the northern lights.

Planning:
Auroras closest to the magnetic pole may be high overhead, but from farther away in Whitehorse and Yellowknife they illuminate the northern horizon as a greenish glow or a faint red. The long nights of autumn and winter provide the longest viewing hours.

Islands of the Arctic

BAFFIN ISLAND

The world's fifth largest island, Baffin is the king of the Canadian Arctic Archipelago. With more than 11,000 residents, it's easily the most populated of the northern isles. It boasts a rich history stretching back to Paleolithic times and was most likely known to the Norsemen of nearby Greenland. Its highest peak, Mount Odin (2,147 metres), is named after the paramount god of Norse mythology. Perched at the island's southern end, Iqaluit is both the capital of Nunavut and an entree to Baffin's many splendours. Yet, the great outdoors is Baffin's main attraction. Scattered around the giant island are eight territorial parks and two large national reserves. A mosaic of rock and ice, east coast Auyuittuq is speckled with glaciers, fjords and dramatic peaks such as Mount Thor, which boasts the globe's greatest sheer vertical drop (1,250 metres). Near the island's northern tip, Sirmilik National Park takes its name from an Inuktitut term meaning "place of many glaciers." Spreading across the Borden Peninsula and adjacent islands, the park is a huge expanse of snowy peaks and glacier-filled valleys that tumble down to bays filled with icebergs. The nearby town of Pond Inlet is the starting point for expeditions into the park and snowmobile or dogsled trips to view Arctic wildlife.

The Legislative Assembly Building in Iqaluit displays a rich collection of Inuit tapestries and carvings, but the town's most distinctive structure is the igloo-shaped St. Jude's Cathedral. The town celebrates the arrival of spring (and daylight) with the annual Toonik Tyme festival in April. Among the many events and activities are ice hockey and ice golf, uphill snowmobile and dogsled races, igloo-building and seal-skinning contests, scavenger hunts, craft markets and copious amounts of traditional local foods.

PLANNING

To reach Baffin Island most people fly to Iqaluit from Montreal, Quebec City or Edmonton. The Unikkaarvik Visitor Centre offers information on exploring the island.

ELLESMERE ISLAND

More like a distant frozen planet than our own Earth, Ellesmere is the northernmost part of Canada. The geography is extreme:

Northwest Passage

Not long after Christopher Columbus discovered that the American landmass was blocking direct trades routes to Asia, Europeans became obsessed with finding a Northwest Passage through the top of the western hemisphere. It proved illusive and in many cases deadly. John Cabot's 1497 voyage on behalf of the English crown is the first recorded attempt to sail around North America via the Arctic. Scores of attempts were launched over the next 400 years, including expeditions by Martin Frobisher, Captain James Cook and Sir John Franklin. The passage was not successfully navigated until Norwegian explorer Roald Amundsen made the journey, and at the time it took him three years, from 1903 to 1906. Given the current climate change and the retreat of polar ice, the Northwest Passage may be more navigable in the future, fulfilling a 500-year-old dream.

vast ice caps and glaciers, dozens of dramatic fjords, and jagged peaks that rise to more than 2,500 metres, some of them so remote they weren't named until the end of the 20th century. Barely a hundred people live in this frozen wilderness, scattered among three tiny communities, including the Canadian Forces Station at Alert—the world's northernmost permanently inhabited settlement. The largest civilian community is Grise Ford, called *Auyuittuq* ("the place that never thaws out") in the local Inuktitut language. Much of the island is protected within the confines of the vast Quttinirpaaq National Park. About one third of the park is covered in glaciers, much of the rest by rugged mountains including the 2,616-metre Mount Barbeau, the highest peak in eastern North America. The park's perpetual light from May to August lends itself to hiking, ski touring and mountaineering, but for only the most experienced cold-weather adventurers.

Getting up close Arctic wildlife, such as polar bears, walruses, seals and narwhals, can be seen at the "flow edge," or the outer rim of floating ice, such as the one near Baffin Island.

PLANNING

Grise Ford and Quttinirpaaq are reached by air from southern Canada via Resolute Bay on Cornwallis Island. Grise Ford is served several times a week by scheduled flights, but reaching Quttinirpaaq requires chartering an aircraft, a more expensive option.

🌲 🎿

VICTORIA ISLAND

The biggest settlement on Victoria Island (not to be confused with Victoria on Vancouver Island) is Cambridge Bay near the island's eastern end. It is en route for vessels travelling the Northwest Passage in the Arctic Ocean. Although a remote outpost was established there in 1921, the town wasn't born until the 1950s, when it was chosen as the site of a Cold War-era Distant Early Warning (DEW) radar station that's still active today. Cambridge Bay has also been tabbed as the future home of Canada's High Arctic Research Station, expected to open in 2017. Among the town's historical relics are the Old Stone Church and the wreck of the *Baymaud*, a schooner used by Roald Amundsen on his 1918–24 polar expeditions and later a Hudson's Bay Company supply vessel. Ovayok (Mount Pelly) Territorial Park

is 15 kilometres east, and home to musk ox, caribou, ptarmigan and other Arctic creatures. Part of the Northwest Territories rather than Nunavut, Ulukhaktok (Holman) on the west side of Victoria Island is renowned for its stone-print artists.

PLANNING

Cambridge Bay is served by regularly scheduled jet flights from Yellowknife and Edmonton. From there, smaller planes ferry passengers to even more isolated Victoria Island communities.

🌲 🏛 🖼 🐋

Stone doorway This *tupqujak* on Baffin Island was built for a shaman to enter the spirit world.

Victoria Island Arctic poppies bloom in a land of rolling tundra and countless lakes, where wildlife is abundant.

Index